LIBRARIES IN HIGHER EDUCATION

LIBRARIES IN HIGHER EDUCATION

the user approach to service

edited by
John Cowley

CLIVE BINGLEY
LONDON

LINNET BOOKS
HAMDEN · CONN

FIRST PUBLISHED 1975 BY CLIVE BINGLEY LTD
16 PEMBRIDGE ROAD LONDON W11
SIMULTANEOUSLY PUBLISHED IN USA BY LINNET BOOKS
AN IMPRINT OF THE SHOE STRING PRESS INC
995 SHERMAN AVENUE HAMDEN CONNECTICUT 06514
SET IN 10 ON 12 POINT PRESS ROMAN
PRINTED AND BOUND IN THE UK BY
REDWOOD BURN LTD TROWBRIDGE AND ESHER
COPYRIGHT © JOHN COWLEY 1975
ALL RIGHTS RESERVED
Clive Bingley ISBN: 0-85157-197-2
Linnet Books ISBN: 0-208-01371-7

Contents

Introduction 1

PART ONE: PROMOTING LIBRARY USE
Chapter 1 The polytechnic background 5
by John Cowley
Chapter 2 Organising for reader services 25
by Gerald Fitzmaurice
Chapter 3 Public relations and publicity 39
by Denis Heathcote
Chapter 4 Non-print media 65
by Ann Aungle
Chapter 5 Teaching library use 83
by Nancy Hammond

PART TWO: SUBJECT SPECIALISATION
Chapter 6 Introduction and survey 105
by Martin Walker
Chapter 7 Book selection 113
by Keith Davis
Chapter 8 Information services for academic staff 125
by Philippa Dolphin
Chapter 9 Planning library instruction 137
by Barbara Penney
Chapter 10 Professional awareness 151
by Martin Walker
Bibliography 159

INTRODUCTION

THE IDEA for this book grew out of the frequently expressed desire of students of librarianship and staff in polytechnic libraries for the presentation of a text which would go some way towards exploring the current development of user services in an academic setting. An additional impetus for the idea came out of the editor's involvement in recent London and Home Counties Management Courses attended by colleagues from overseas. It became clear during these sessions that American librarians in particular were anxious to know more of library practice in the new polytechnics and to understand something of the background of these institutions.

Subsequently, some of my colleagues at the Polytechnic of North London agreed to write about their work or that part of it concerned with service to the user. No attempt has been made to present a study of library administration, and reference to systems and organisation is only incidental to the main purpose of the book. At suitable points in the text practice in British and American university libraries is contrasted with that in polytechnics.

The first chapter outlines the development and organisation of the polytechnics and their libraries. Then follows a brief outline of the development of user services. A great deal of the material in this concluding section is discussed in more detail in subsequent chapters.

Chapter two examines the organisational base from which satisfactory user services can be launched. It discusses possible conflicts inherent in the wide and demanding job description of the subject specialist and has something to say on job satisfaction for the young professional graduate librarian.

Denis Heathcote then discusses the importance of good public relations between the librarian and the user and examines the quality of library publications, with examples drawn from both American and British libraries. In her chapter on the non-book media, Ann Aungle outlines organisational problems and stresses the importance of the library's role in the building of effective media resources in the academic institution. This section of the book is concluded by Nancy Hammond's chapter on the planning of library education in which she gives examples of actual approaches to teaching method.

In the final section of the book, four subject specialists jointly present views on various aspects of their work, including library instruction, information services, stock exploitation and, importantly, their attitudes to professional awareness which might be described as the attempt to prepare thoroughly for the variety of duties facing the subject specialist in the academic library.

The book has been written by librarians currently engaged in the development of a library which will double in size during the decade and which is committed to a programme of maximum exploitation of resources in physical surroundings which are far from ideal. We hope that those at present engaged in similar work, together with students of academic librarianship, will find within the pages some measure of inspiration and guidance for the future.

PART 1

Promoting library use

CHAPTER I

The polytechnic background

John Cowley

Purpose and aims
FACED WITH the problem of expanding higher education, the government in the mid-sixties noted the advanced work being carried out in a large number of regional and area colleges, and decided that the future of these institutions did not lie in their development as universities but as higher education establishments having their own distinctive character within the local education sector. These ideas were officially presented in May 1966 in the white paper *A plan for polytechnics and other colleges* which stressed the need for the creation of a new kind of higher education institution, significantly different from the existing universities. It also asked for the future concentration of these resources in a limited number of strong centres. The intention was to create a 'separate but equal' local authority sector of higher education bearing a strong interest in vocationally orientated, interdisciplinary courses.

The polytechnics were to have a student body drawn from wider age and social ranges and a span of courses which would include work below the first degree level. Research and higher degrees would be accommodated in the polytechnics, particularly work having direct application to the needs of industry, business and the professions. Both socially and academically, the student body would be more wide ranging than in the universities. One advantage in offering this breadth of activity was seen to be the real possibility of student transfer from one course to another. Flexibility within the polytechnics was to help solve the problem of student wastage experienced in the universities and colleges of education.

The provision of common first year studies for honours and ordinary degree courses and the possibility of transfer to and from HND studies were designed to assist the student in finding the right course at the right level. Varied patterns of attendance were also to be helpful in enabling a student to attend his course in a way convenient to his private circumstances.

The white paper saw the polytechnics primarily as teaching institutions, stating that efforts would be concentrated on the development and application of 'what is known' towards the fulfilment of the personal and professional concerns of their students and the solution of industrial and social problems. Some courses were to be linked with traditional local needs of industry and commerce and devised in consultation with specialist needs.

The first major statement by a politician on the new polytechnics came in the much quoted 'Woolwich' speech of Anthony Crosland, the Secretary of State for Education and Science. He pointed to the findings of the Robbins Committee that 'Higher Education is so obviously and rightly of public concern . . . that it is difficult to defend the continued absence of coordinated principles and of a general conception of objectives'. He saw the solution in the creation of a system based on the autonomous sector, represented by the universities, and on the public sector, represented by the leading technical colleges. Crosland strongly supported the idea of this dual, or binary system which allowed each sector to make its distinctive contribution and contrasted it favourably with the alternative unitary system 'hierarchically arranged on the ladder principle' with the universities at the top and the other institutions down below. Such a system he saw as an educational rat race during which the needs of society were forgotten and which ignored the diverse needs of the full range of potential students. He implied that the traditional methods of teaching and course organisation in the universities was not sufficiently flexible to meet an increasing demand for vocational and professional courses which had developed in society. Crosland therefore, looked to a new, more diversified, sector to provide the appropriate attitudes and outlook conducive to change in higher education. The political interests of the Labour Party led them to seek a greater measure of social control for a substantial part of higher education, this to be achieved by local authority involvement.

The secretary envisaged the public sector taking the lead in the development of a wide range of professionally based courses serving the growing needs of those in social work, business and commerce, librarianship and related areas. He advocated a re-examination of traditional curricula which he hoped would lead to a change of emphasis and style without any loss of quality. He was most anxious that the polytechnics should not feebly imitate provision in the universities. Basically, Crosland was looking for a distinctive excellence and new approaches geared to meet society's needs.

The furore surrounding the Woolwich speech led Crosland to return to the theme in 1967 at Lancaster. There he pointed out that he had not invented the plural, or binary, system. A great deal of higher education was already being carried out in the public sector and his intention was to strengthen this area rather than to pour all resources into the universities. It was good, he said, to avoid a monopoly situation in higher education and thought 'a variety of institutions under different control a wiser investment for the future'. He was also at pains to point out that the public sector was better equipped to offer help to those students who did not want a degree course, but who preferred a shorter course leading to, say, a professional diploma. He also considered that the range of courses available in the colleges would help to cater for the student who began his studies at less than degree level, but who might respond to the stimulus of his course by transferring to one of the new degree courses offered in the same institution. Early leavers and late developers could benefit from the polytechnic system which was sufficiently comprehensive as to provide students at different levels of attainment with a range of choices and an alternative route.

Shirley Williams, Under-Secretary of State, strongly supported the Crosland viewpoint. Presenting her views at Coombe Lodge, she, too, stressed the theme of the polytechnic as a comprehensive institution, having a combination of full time, part-time and sandwich students taking courses at degree and sub-degree level. She stressed the importance of the continuation of part-time courses and challenged the sanctity of the standard full-time, three year first degree. The traditional university education end-on to secondary school she saw as far from ideal for many students and advocated instead education as a life long process. She concluded that the 'intermingling, educationally and socially, of full-time and part-time, younger and older students' would give the polytechnics their unique character.

7

Those academics already in the polytechnic sector tended to demonstrate substantial agreement with the Crosland-Williams viewpoint. J A P Hall, of Hatfield, expressed the view that polytechnic education should be student centred and community orientated, with course content and patterns established in accordance with student and social needs. He, too, advocated the creation of a network of life long refresher and re-education courses, which largely avoided the narrow treatment of subject disciplines. He also maintained that research and consultancy in the polytechnics should be aimed at solving the practical problems. Dr Brosan, now of North East London, stressed that the polytechnics had to make the utilisation of knowledge as respectable and as widespread as the acquisition of knowledge. He challenged the value of the total commitment to conventional academic disciplines which might be seen as artificial devices constructed to provide a traditional, academic framework. There should be, instead, some attempt made to place learning and knowledge within the context of the vocational setting.

Thus the practical and flexible nature of the polytechnics was seen by many to be in contrast with the traditional university concepts and standards. The advocates of polytechnic education saw them as institutions of education satisfying the more utilitarian demands of society, contributing directly and intentionally to the pressing and practical purposes of society.

With the benefit of hindsight, it is now possible to advance rather more cautious views concerning the role of polytechnics. There has been a tendency in the early seventies for polytechnics to convert many of the old diploma courses into first degree courses. While it is true that many polytechnics have continued to offer original patterns of attendance and a firm interest in sandwich, modular and inter disciplinary courses, it is also the case that there is a strong element of the traditional in the polytechnics, which in many ways is a response to student demands and the conservation of the many social forces influencing the development of the new institutions. In any case, the universities have not remained unchanging. During the last twenty five years, decisions surrounding university function have been made within the context of quantitative expansion, student militancy, the questioning of curricula and the debating of the main aims of higher education. Opinions as to what knowledge is worth possessing have had great influence on curricula and methods of teaching. Patterns of development within higher education have emerged as a result of its relation with society. The growth in demand and the implication of the Robbins Report brought the whole of higher education under scrutiny, and it was not only in the polytechnics that socio-economic pressures were to create change.

However, it is possible to point to some major differences between the university and the public sector. The polytechnics are different in that they: 1 are not financed by the University Grants Commission, 2 do not possess a royal charter to award their own degrees, and 3 have not, as yet, had any clear guidance on the part research must play in the life of the colleges, and it is useful to examine these factors in a little more detail.

Finance and control

The University Grants Commission was first formed in 1919, under the control of the treasury, to act as a buffer between the universities and the state. In the early years, the funds distributed were small, but after the second world war the finances involved became substantial and the UGC increasingly exercised an influence over university planning. While the universities themselves generate and take steps to accomplish their policies, the UGC has had its powers widened 'to assist, in consultation with the universities and other bodies concerned, the preparation and execution of such plans for the development of the universities . . . in order to ensure that they are fully adequate to national needs'. However, the commission still aims to avoid direct government intervention in the running of universities; instead, it formulates overall strategy, but allows considerable freedom within the approved framework. Departures from UGC principles can be discouraged by withdrawal of financial support. Acceptable strategy is communicated by 'memoranda of guidance' which indicate developments likely to gain support. The UGC also closely controls capital expenditure with grants given for specific buildings with cost limits closely defined. Seventy five percent of recurrent expenditure and ninety percent of capital expenditure is supplied out of public funds. The recurrent grant, once allocated, is not ear marked for specific purposes but is subject to guidance from the UGC. It is important to note that university finance operates on a five year cycle, which system offers possibilities for rational planning, admittedly somewhat undermined in recent times by unexpectedly heavy inflation. This quinquennial system however does encourage sensible forward planning, with proper thought given to demand and capacity in the universities.

Expenditure in the polytechnics, on the other hand, is determined by the individual authorities who have to relate educational needs to the availability of money from local rates and the rate support grant. Both current and capital expenditure derive from the same source, although the Department of Education and Science controls the starts in a given year. Expenditure on advanced courses is administered through a pooling system whereby every authority contributes its share to an FE pool, from which the providers of local higher education recover their actual expenditure. The system is justified in the sense that polytechnics, like the universities, recruit nationally, and pooling is used to remove the hardship caused by the local education authority having to bear the full cost of the courses, the benefit of which is felt by students drawn from many quarters. To meet criticism of the system, a pooling committee was set up in 1967. This has no executive powers but gives fair consideration to financial problems arising from the system. The year to year basis of polytechnic finance also presents major problems and probably results in a good deal of piecemeal planning. The situation is further complicated by the fact that the rate support grant is negotiated for a two year period only.

The greater degree of freedom enjoyed by the universities in relation to finance is also reflected in their greater measure of administrative autonomy. The polytechnics are answerable substantially to the controlling local education authority, while the universities are more concerned with internal moderation brought about by competing interests within their own walls. The universities are able to launch new courses and award degrees with considerable freedom, just as long as the new ideas do not seriously conflict with UGC principles. Public sector developments on the other hand, involve scrutiny by the local education authority, regional bodies, the Department of Education and Science and the Council for National Academic Awards. The polytechnics have to overcome many hurdles before bringing a proposed course to fruition, and, as many critics of the binary system have pointed out, there is as yet no machinery for coordinating university and polytechnic course planning either at regional or national level.

Council for National Academic Awards
The Council for National Academic Awards, established by royal charter in 1964, has been a major force in establishing the polytechnics as viable institutions of higher education. The council awards first, higher and research degrees, all of which are accepted as being fully equivalent to a university degree of a similar level. The council must be satisfied about educational standards, but col-

leges are free to devise their own curricula and syllabi, to examine students with the help of external examiners approved by the council, and to settle their own admission qualifications. This latter point has enabled some polytechnics to move away from the rigid adherence to entry by means of 'A' levels, and recruitment for courses, such as the BA Sociology of Education at Middlesex Polytechnic, draw on mature students whose experience is seen to be more important than mere possession of the standard two or three 'A' levels.

During the early years of development, the CNAA had much to do with the creation of parity between polytechnics and the universities. Its insistence on high academic standards did much to remove prejudice against the polytechnics. In the formative years employers and career advisers were dubious of the polytechnics and their new courses, but the work of the CNAA helped to bring about a change of heart. By also encouraging others to devise their own courses, the council helped to remove the straight jacket of the old London external degree courses, which, until the late sixties, held too firm a grip on the local authority sector of higher education. A further important aspect of the council's work was its insistence on improved support facilities, including libraries. Submission for new courses frequently led to a conditional approval which involved the strengthening of both teaching staff and library facilities. In the early days of the polytechnics, the recommended standards for libraries quoted by the CNAA did much to improve what were abysmally low level services, and although these standards are now withdrawn their existence in the formative years was a boon to deprived colleges.

Now the mood is for further change in the sense that the council is preparing the ground to give greater autonomy to the more advanced polytechnics. It is possible that departments of proven quality will be given more freedom to launch new courses. Martin Trow foresaw this development when he advocated the control of an external authority only for as long as was necessary for the polytechnics to develop their own style and standards. He suggested 'once the forces for change are established then outside control is best put aside'. The present indications are that the CNAA will be highly selective in the gradual releasing of powers of validation, even to the extent of granting full powers to one faculty while denying it to another in the same polytechnic. Trow sees a real dilemma arising from the polytechnics' move towards autonomy. On the one hand, the ambitious and solid experience of the academic staff are leading the way towards greater academic freedom. On the other, the complex web of controls administered by various outside agencies inevitably creates tensions and frustrations for staff who are becoming more and more confident in their abilities to create and present high level courses. Unless the polytechnics are given greater freedom, it is argued that the resultant tension and frustration will lead to loss of morale and the draining away of the best energies. It is probable that such problems will be solved very gradually with the evolution of each polytechnic proceeding at a rate somewhat at variance to that of similar institutions. The same can be said of the progress in the development of polytechnic libraries which we shall consider later in some detail.

Research

The place of research in the polytechnics is still the cause of considerable controversy. The early stress on the importance of teaching, and the lack of research traditions and appropriate funding in most polytechnics has created an uneasy situation which continues to create problems. As early as 1967 a statement in parliament indicated that it would be necessary to make provision in the polytechnics for research essential to the proper fulfilment of the teaching functions and 'the maintenance and development of close links with industry, particularly local industry, so as to promote the rapid allocation of the results of research to its problems'. The strong interest in sandwich courses and the special relationship enjoyed by many polytechnic departments with local industrial and commercial concerns suggested that such statements were more than pious hopes. In the event, the amount of research carried out has been very little compared with that in the universities, but where research programmes of substance do exist, this has carried major implications for the polytechnic and its library in terms of resources and manpower.

The current situation

It is, of course, too early to assess the significance and uniqueness of the polytechnics in higher education, but it appears that many of the pioneering thoughts of politicians and educationalists recorded in the late sixties must now be seriously challenged. Not only are student number targets being constantly adjusted downwards, but also the type of work being done in the polytechnics is rapidly being adjusted to meet consumer demands. Just as the universities have become increasingly concerned with technological, vocational and managerial courses, so the polytechnics have become increasingly arts minded. The real growth in the public sector is in the social science, humanities and fine arts area. Although the structural and financial features in the public sector continue to differentiate the polytechnics from the universities, in academic terms distinctions are becoming less clear. Students can read classics at a polytechnic and study brewing at university. If this trend continues, it strengthens the case of those who argue for an end to the binary policy and the creation of an instrument of national planning and coordination for higher education.

If, on the other hand, those concerned with polytechnics see them as substantially different from the universities, with a special socio-educational role to perform, as do Pratt and Burgess, then a firmer policy will have to be developed. Clearer directives and an appropriate level of financial and resource allocation would be needed. Crosland's desire to discover coordinating principles and a conception of objectives, to encourage comprehensiveness and a greater measure of social control, have not been realised. The signs are there of piecemeal development and a lack of rationale. Importantly, for those currently involved in polytechnic work either as student or teacher, the continuing lack of resources constantly undermines the quality of polytechnic activity, not least in relation to the services and functions of the libraries.

The polytechnic libraries

With hardly any exceptions, the polytechnic libraries, like their parent institutions, have developed from small, scattered, under financed and under staffed beginnings. In general, local authorities in the early sixties were happy to provide minimal low cost services, and there was little pressure from educationalists or teaching staff for the provision of even adequate library services. This situation was underlined by the way in which many technical college librarians viewed with some amazement the battle for resources waged by Gordon Wright in Hertfordshire. Consequently, the transition from technical college standards to a level appropriate to the needs of the new polytechnics involved the adoption of fresh attitudes, the creation of new policies, and a vast increase in allocation of resources to the library. This growth and development in the libraries came at a time when other interests in the polytechnics were rightly fighting for their bigger share of the cake. In the eyes of many the library was seen to be something of a fringe luxury, a service to be developed when all other matters had been put right. However, the firmer DES interest in polytechnics, the CNAA's concern for standards and the example of a few enlightened authorities, combined with student and academic pressure to bring about a better state of affairs. The Library Association issued its first standards for polytechnic libraries in

1968 and the Council of Polytechnic Librarians has exercised a continuous watching brief over affairs in the seventies. The net result has been a major upgrading of services, with substantial increases in bookfunds and resources. The situation is still markedly uneven, and, just as James Thompson comments on the variations in university library administration, instancing a 2.2 percent of total expenditure at Birmingham compared with 7.1 percent at Warwick, so the situation varies in the polytechnics. Several, including the Polytechnic of North London, Hatfield and Newcastle, can now boast expenditure at the rate of six percent of the total, while some of the less fortunate still spend less than three percent of income. Bookfunds have generally increased dramatically and not less than six of the thirty polytechnics are currently spending over £100,000 per annum on new bookstock. This compares with constituent college expenditures in the sixties of around £3000 per annum. David Bagley quotes the example of the eighteen regional colleges which, in 1964/65, had bookstocks averaging 18,000 and bookfunds of only £5000. Library staffs, too, have grown, and this has offered real opportunities for the re-structuring and development of services. North London had a total staff of thirty in 1972, but by 1974 this figure had grown to fifty-five. Perhaps the greatest disappointment in the last five years has been the comparative lack of progress with new buildings. Although there have been encouraging developments at Hatfield, Newcastle and Lanchester, most of the polytechnics continue to house their library services in limited space in old buildings, often scattered between a collection of sites. This split site problem continues to absorb wastefully a substantial proportion of staff and stock resources which could be much better utilised given single site operations.

In one important essential, then, polytechnics are in great contrast to the universities; they have suffered from seriously inadequate library facilities. Recent progress apart, it is still fair to say the Crosland's 'parity of esteem' will remain something of a myth unless the material resources of the polytechnics can be further improved. Academic staff lack adequate support services and have to work in crowded conditions for lower salaries, and these deficiencies spill over in to the library sector.

Particular sufferers as a result of this low level of provision are, of course, the students. Their militant action in February 1971, when most polytechnic libraries were occupied for the day, came as no surprise. Dr R F Robbins, at the time, spoke fervently for the urgent priority of library improvement, and critics of the situation no doubt had in mind the average twenty or thirty books provided for each polytechnic student as contrasted with the 150 mentioned in the Parry Report as suitable for a student in an established university. Mike Terry, an executive member of the NUS, speaking of student protest in the polytechnics, blamed the government for launching a massive polytechnic programme without allocating adequate capital for development.

Although the current economic position justifies little optimism, it is true to say that since the late sixties there has been some improvement in the situation. The CNAA's attention to the infrastructure and the greater pressure from within the new institutions have combined to create improvements in the college environment and supporting services. Many polytechnic libraries are now able to offer much more sophistication of service, a greater measure of reader assistance and fast growing bookstocks. There is clearly a definite move towards the realisation of the CNAA statement of 1965 which stressed that library facilities and services should be designed to meet fully the needs of students and teaching staff, and would provide 'a wide and up-to-date- coverage of the subjects of the proposed degree courses' to the extent that students should not have 'to rely upon external library provision to fulfil their requirements'.

The development of reader services
Subject specialisation. Given that library resources are bound to improve in the next decade, it is well worth considering the opportunities available to polytechnic library staff for developing services to the users. It is important to ensure that academic staff and students of departments come to view the library as a natural centre for study, information and research, and that they receive a highly personal service despite the substantial growth in size of the library. At North London we take the view that these aims can best be realised through the availability of a subject specialist librarian adequately supported by small teams of senior staff having functional and coordinating responsibilities. Their task is to forge extremely strong links between the library and the various teaching groups and departments. A great deal of recent experience in the new universities and the polytechnics suggests that the most effective way of establishing a good liaison with users is through the work of a strong, highly motivated team of graduate specialist librarians who concentrate a great deal of their energies within a carefully selected subject area. Each specialist has the responsibility for 'maximising the use of the library's resources in his area', as Holbrook puts it. Normally, the staff have at least a first degree in an appropriate subject together with post-graduate qualifications and

15

experience in librarianship. He or she is well versed in educational aims and methods of teaching and is expected to familiarize himself with the work of the department with which he is associated. The job description varies in detail from place to place, but, as the idea of full integration is pursued, the subject specialist's work includes book selection in cooperation with academic staff, advice on the classification of stock, the offering of current awareness and information services, the close study of the needs of staff and students, individual and group instruction in library use, participation in reader advisory services, including work at the information desk, and, in general, the fullest exploitation of stock within the selected area of operations. All these activities are ideally linked with some measure of involvement in the day to day administration of the library, and the training and supervision of support staff. Contact with each other, even when the split-site situation creates difficulties, is essential in terms of a regular exchange of ideas and the creation of a team approach to the tasks at hand. It is important not to allow specialisation to lead to isolation. Contact is also maintained through liaison with senior staff, particularly when the latter have a coordinating function to fulfil.

The subject specialists relation with a department will ideally be thorough and informal, and it is important that the librarian has a place on the departmental boards of studies and similar bodies. The exploration of the detail of library provision and an intelligent approach to forward planning will depend on the success of the subject specialist in establishing a real rapport with his academic colleagues. Whether information is exchanged in the library, over coffee, or at the departmental meeting is irrelevant; what is important, is that the department understands the full potential of the library and the way in which it can respond to needs. Holbrook stresses that the library subject specialist should have the opportunity 'to advise on the impact on the library of changes in student numbers; of the introduction of new courses and options; and of new interdisciplinary or modular courses'. He also rightly stresses the importance to the library of knowledge of changes in teaching methods, reductions in class contact hours and increases in assessed work. Many librarians have experienced the impact on the library of the introduction of greater levels of project work which created unprecedented demands on the limited resources of the parent library. Without the necessary planning and consultation between librarian and academic staff, considerable frustration can result.

It has to be admitted that subject specialisation has not always worked. Ralph Ellsworth's description of the weak minded librarian caught between philosophical forces presents an unhappy picture of inter disciplinary confusion. There is no doubt that the physical splitting of bookstock around a number of sites, combined with the interest in cross discipline activity, which is a feature of many modern degree courses, does create problems of choice of location for material. However, the work of the subject specialist, with its stress on close liaison with departments and programmes of library education, is designed to overcome this kind of problem. In any case, it is well known that pressure from academic staff over the exact and most appropriate location and usage of material is an old problem which has tested librarians for many years, and is not necessarily related to the concept of subject specialist activity. Leicester University's abandonment of subject specialisation on the grounds of lack of coordination of work with the resultant 'incoherence, disunity and confusion' leaves aside the question of a senior coordinating influence, effective team training, and techniques of library management which could be used to eliminate these problems. Guttsman, an advocate of subject specialisation, rightly raises problems of organisational structure and control and the possible dysfunctional impact of subject specialisation, but considers that on balance it offers a better service to users where they number between 3000-8000.

Library instruction. Closely related to the other work of the subject specialist is that of training or instructing the library user, or library orientation, as the Americans prefer. Students should receive guidance and instruction sufficient to enable them to exploit the full potential of the resources of books and information available to them. It is my view, having experienced work as a tutor librarian within the excellent pioneering period in Hertfordshire in the fifties and sixties, that at the undergraduate level this instruction is ideally provided by the subject specialist librarians, who relate this aspect of their work to all the other activities coming under the heading of liaison with and service to a department. Library instruction involves the closest cooperation with academic colleagues. Despite the length of time it has been around, it is still not widely accepted as a legitimate part of the librarian's work by many academic staff, but a level of persistence, combined with careful preparation and a modicum of teaching skills, can lead to initial exercises in library instruction which will impress upon staff and students the value of this work. There is no reason why this type of teaching should not be built into a degree course to the extent that there could be a joint assessment of a student's bibliographical skills and subject knowledge within the context of project work.

A COPOL document (1972) suggests that 'The amount of instruction should be adequate enough to give every student a thorough introduction to the library and its resources, and should be later augmented by further periods of more sophisticated instruction closely related to the student's academic work'. It is also possible to allow students on sandwich courses to bring actual information problems from real working situations, thus creating a source of purpose in their library course activities. A final point to remember in relation to library instruction is the value of such activity when it is related to the needs of academic staff. Where a polytechnic organises orientation courses for new staff, it should be arranged that the potential of the library services is explained to them. It is also useful to consider inviting staff to training sessions designed to put over the use of a major bibliographical service such as the *Science citation index*. There are also opportunities for librarians and academic staff to join forces in the presentation of a course of library instruction, and individual or small group work with research staff can carry substantial benefits for personnel embarking on a major study in depth, perhaps for the first time.

Information and library publications. Further useful exploitation of stock can arise from the existence of a variety of information services available to users. Current awareness and contents page services, whether home produced or obtained commercially, form a useful aspect of library provision. Knowledge of research and teaching requirements and the creation of reader profiles, should enable the librarian to supply academic staff with information of real interest. The specialist librarian, knowing of his academic colleagues' needs, which are often very specific, can help him trace and obtain currently important literature. This implies the closest liaison between the librarian and the teacher and a considerable investment of time on the part of the librarian. However, the benefits are not one sided in that the flow of information between the two participants can add greatly to the librarian's appreciation of the subject and can have a beneficial impact on the quality of the bookstock.

A further aspect of service to readers which has been marked over the years by lack of effort and a paucity of ideas has been that of library publications. Both the content of library productions and the quality of the art work have left a great deal to be desired. It is my belief that, given an adequate standard of presentation and a proper assessment of content and detail, an attractive library guide and a mix of other special publications will justify the time and money spent on them. How a user absorbs his knowledge of the library will depend a great deal on his personality and tastes, but there seems to be evidence available to suggest that a concise library guide in a student's folder will usefully remind him of the services available. The production of current awareness bulletins and specialist annotated reading lists, ideally planned in conjunction with academic colleagues, can be of real assistance to the student. Unattractive stencilled handouts are probably a waste of time, but a well produced item, suitably timed, and issued within the context of total package of student assistance, can encourage heavy and effective use of library resources.

Non print media services. A combination of factors have encouraged the idea of a strong development within the polytechnics of non print media services. Lack of space, earlier deficiencies of stock, the absence of substantial retrospective collections of journals, and the upsurge of interest in educational technology and new methods of teaching, in many cases brought about through the success of the Open University, have continued to awaken interest in this sector of library activity. The traditional view of libraries as collections of books is long since relegated to history and the increasing production and use of the non book media makes it essential for libraries to equip themselves accordingly. Indeed, such has been the impact in some quarters that the learning resource centre has become the overriding concept, relegating the library, as such, to an apparently insignificant place in the total organisation. One suspects that these early difficulties with nomenclature, organisation and structure are passing aberrations, for no matter how things are set up and despite the variety of names given to the units, the library must be bound up with the provision of this media. The physical form of publication is largely immaterial. The critical factor is the value of the item as a source of learning or teaching to the parent institution. The library will inevitably be bound up with the acquisition, storage, indexing and retrieval of the various media, ranging from books to videotapes, and it can also encourage the use of this material by demonstration, display, exploitation and promotional exercises. A great deal of incidental knowledge of the scope and use of non book media can be instilled during the periods of library instruction, during which students can be asked to use tapes, microforms and other media.

The library is ideally placed to arrange the issue and recall of materials and should provide extensive facilities within its own walls for the use of these aids. The typical polytechnic would expect to provide listening and viewing facilities involving the possible use of study carrels, induction loops and special desk top services. A polytechnic library suitably attuned to new developments will have in its stock a collection of records, tapes, slides, films, learning programmes and microforms. The aim will be to provide a learning resource centre containing a range of recorded knowledge in a variety of physical forms.

In a library situation of acute shortage of space, one common to nearly all the polytechnics, the microform takes on a new importance. The increased flow of micro publication, combined with the quality of the latest micro reading equipment, should overcome the reader resistance to the use of microforms. Long runs of journals required in the polytechnics for new degree courses and research activity can usefully be purchased in microform. The user, not least the librarian himself, prefers to work from hard copy, but given the special circumstances facing the polytechnics, this particular aspect of media provision should be exploited to the full.

User facilities. While discussing the problem of presenting an adequate service to the polytechnic library user, the significance of the needs of the various groups of clientele cannot be ignored. The requirements of the undergraduate, the research worker, the academic or the administrator are frequently disparate. Early statements about the role of the polytechnics stressed the importance of the teaching function and it is true to say that a great deal of effort has been directed towards providing a service to the undergraduate. While individual needs vary the basic requirements of the undergraduate would seem to consist of: a) comfortable and adequate study facilities, b) long hours of opening, c) a substantial, well-chosen bookstock, augmented by periodicals, d) basic reference and information services, e) a flexible issue system, backed by speedy inter library loans, reservation and request systems, f) special undergraduate collections of key material, g) instruction in library use, linked with a high quality personal service at the enquiry desk and a supply of carefully prepared library publications.

It is outside the scope of this book to deliberate at length on some of these points. Suffice it to say that seating on a 1:4 or 1:5 basis is the target set by many polytechnic libraries to meet the needs of the student body. Libraries should be open at least twelve hours a day, and weekend opening should be considered in relation to staff availability and student demand. Pleasant, comfortable and varied study surroundings should be provided to counter the frequently poor home or lodging circumstances of many students. Polytechnic provision of student halls of residence is notoriously deficient, this being another aspect of deficiencies in the public sector compared with what is available at many universities. Consequently, adequate library, study and canteen facilities can take on a new significance for the polytechnic student.

Discussion of the work of the subject specialists has already underlined the importance of an adequate provision of books and other library materials. Given this level of provision, the remaining significant point deserving of a great deal of attention is the quality of service and measure of exploitation to be offered. A simple issue system as employed in a typical public library is not appropriate for the academic library. Undergraduates will normally be allowed to borrow about six books at a time for a period of a month, but it is important to arrange shorter or longer periods of loan for different categories of material for students involved in different types of study. The student of education may wish to borrow classroom materials or a project collection for the period of his attachment to a school, while a group of students asked to read a key chapter of a book may be happy to have a one day or a four hour loan period; a a sufficient time to extract what is needed before handing on the item to a fellow student. The variety of systems applied to meet student needs and the possible limitations of stock can be costly to administer in terms of staff time and clerical work, but the end product is a quality service which students see to be equitable and helpful.

The provision of undergraduate collections of books and offprints can be an immense boon to the young student who should complete his course having had access to books, journals and other media sufficient to meet his reasonable demands. The dangers inherent in providing such a service largely centre on the extra staffing required and a possible wastage of stock where bad choices are made and insufficient weeding is carried out. Ideally, the undergraduate collection should be relatively small and always current. Once again, the fullest cooperation is required between lecturer and librarian, so that the right quantities can be put aside to meet particular situations, and well calculated periods of time allowed for retention in the collection. Many books can be returned to normal open shelves after a relatively short period, while reasonable advance notice of need should be given to the librarian if he is to be able to collect material together in time.

The existence of significant pockets of research activity in a polytechnic, as is the case in the Polytechnic of North London, carries with it the need for substantial library expenditure on research materials, particularly journals and associated abstracting and indexing services. The actual amount to be spent on research as opposed to teaching areas is by no means easy to calculate. Given that all the polytechnics are busily endeavouring to build up adequate bookstocks for basic teaching needs, the expending of funds on research materials can be regarded as a further embarrassment in an already under financed situation. Fortunately, there is degree of overlap in the work of final year undergraduates, research staff and the preparation of teaching to the extent that expenditure on research materials can be justified. Service to the research worker must take into account his needs for a generous supply of materials and a greater measure of use of information services, inter library loans and access to other institutions. The typical researcher will require a larger number of books for longer periods and would benefit from the availability of a study carrel for extensive periods. Teaching staff should also receive a very sophisticated service, unhindered by too many petty rules. Ideally, the lecturer in a particular department should have the services of a subject specialist able to understand his basic requirements, and for the two of them to be constantly in touch with each other concerning additions to stock and services to students.

Summary

Polytechnic libraries are in a stage of rapid development. Increased resources are being made available to them, and they have left behind the period of small scale operations and minimum provision. Most of the polytechnic librarians are producing or have produced development plans, which not only put the case for more space and better buildings, but also describe the rationale behind the redevelopment of staff and improvement of services. A great deal of thought has gone into the investigation of basic objectives and the relationship between the library and the polytechnic it serves. The nature of the teaching, the content of courses and the make-up of the library clientele, serve to influence the nature of the library. The interaction of librarians with students, research workers and academic colleagues is helping to create a substantially new type of library milieu. A large measure of effort is being directed towards the development of liaison between the library and other elements of the polytechnic, mainly through the work of the subject specialist teams and senior co-ordinating staff. Considerable importance is attached to the maximum utilisation of resources which, perforce, must be limited, and librarians must bear in mind links with the computer and developments in education technology.

The remaining chapters of this book will present the views and experience of a number of colleagues who have worked with me during a period of rapid development at the Polytechnic of North London. Their writings are based both on experience gained in our own polytechnic and on a study of activity in other academic libraries. Experience tends to show that to some extent developments in the new polytechnic libraries are running a varied course, but throughout the thirty institutions there appears to be in progress a search for a rationale at the centre of which is a real desire to develop reader services. The aim at North London is to create a homogeneous service whose broad aims and policy constantly evolve under the guidance of a central team of senior staff. On the other hand, I hope the succeeding chapters will demonstrate that individual members of the professional team, whether operating as a coordinator, a site librarian, or a subject specialist, are able to give expression to their individuality and respond sensitively to local situations within the context of defined aims of the system as a whole.

CHAPTER II

Organising for reader services

Gerald Fitzmaurice

STEERING COMMITTEE PAPER No 18 (SC18) of the Cambridge Library Management Research Unit (CLMRU) remarks upon the need to relate resource allocation to the objectives of libraries. A primary question in analysing the redistribution of resources is 'which objectives should be more fully satisfied?'.

The purpose of this volume is to reassert the position of reader services as the primary service area in polytechnic libraries and that therefore they should have a concentration of resources in terms of staff, equipment and time; and that all other library services should be organised in such a way as to allow maximum effort to be directed to reader services. This paper will try to show that in order to achieve this situation, the right conditions must exist. In polytechnic libraries this will probably mean a reorganisation of both staff structure and technical services, in order to release resources which would otherwise be wasted. These resources can then be used to produce more efficient reader services. In the first few years of their lives polytechnic libraries, as has been mentioned in the previous chapter, have done no more than establish basic library stocks, minimum levels of staffing and limited accommodation.

The intention of this paper is to indicate some ways in which polytechnic libraries, in order to cope with their historical legacy of poor buildings and split sites, the newly emerging professional manpower problem and the growth of centralised services can take short cuts by streamlining their procedures. For example they can use centralised services or farm out routine work with, if necessary, a resultant loss in the 'quality' of technical output. Much, if not all, of core technical service work is repetitive in its on-going procedures and inefficient in its effects; it is doubtful whether the results of localised cataloguing are more 'beneficial' to the average polytechnic library user than those of centralised services which use uniform and established systems. There will be occasions when the peculiarities of a local system can only be catered for by local professionalism and expertise but such instances are rare.

A basic difference between the newer university libraries and many polytechnic libraries lies in the physically diversified units making up the latter and the resource disadvantages, such as the need to duplicate, which result from this. Shirley Williams' statement that 'the mainspring of the polytechnic policy was the need to concentrate scarce teaching resources and expensive advanced equipment on certain centres of high level work, rather than disposing them effectively across a multiplicity of individual colleges' did not, however, bring many of these individual colleges physically together and this became one of the fundamental limiting factors in the effective growth of polytechnic libraries. Despite Shirley Williams' idea of concentrating resources, most polytechnics are located on unplanned sites, generally dispersed in inner city areas. Liverpool and inner London are notorious examples of this. Many of these polytechnics would like to have a central campus site, preferably in a green belt area although this would remove them from the areas they were originally intended to serve. Ian Brown in the *Higher education review* argues for the retention of polytechnics in dispersed locations in conurbations rather than in the country on single sites. Replacement in the cities is too expensive at the moment; the compromise could probably be summarised as 'adaptation with ingenuity'. There is no clear government thought on multi-site policies. No case for single site areas is made in Design Note No 8: 'a polytechnic should remain as an integral part of the community and this may be done better by staying in the heart of an urban area—perhaps even on single sites'.

So, from a library point of view, polytechnics are not only a coming together of service points, but also an amalgamation of different technical systems and styles of staff utilisation. It should be remembered that many polytechnics linked a college of technology and a college of art. The former probably already pursued Shirley Williams' idea that 'teachers of advanced work need to undertake some research so that they can keep abreast of their own subjects . . . polytechnics in some cases will want to undertake research for industries in their areas'. A tradition of research, similar to that of the universities, was already strong in some polytechnics, especially in the applied sciences. The government's policy on teaching excellence, an idea emphatically stated by Margaret Thatcher; 'polytechnics should be first and foremost centres of teaching excellence', did not need stressing as many of the old constituent colleges already had excellent teaching departments. The major difficulty was the need to achieve the right balance between teaching and research which the library and other areas could then effectively serve. Polytechnics are in a difficult transitional period, not knowing whether to keep to their original teaching function or to push further into the research field. This situation will obviously affect the way in which a library defines its objectives: it may not be sure how it should organise in order to serve the differing aims of teaching and research. Library objectives are bound to change in relation to developing user needs and there does seem to be a movement, now fortified by CNAA pronouncement, towards pursuing more research in the polytechnics. But, whatever the advantages of relating resource allocation to the general and specific objectives of libraries, in polytechnic libraries the limited nature of these resources result in a service which is frequently below standard.

The two possible strategies for dealing with this situation are a restructuring of staff and the more intensive use of centralised services. The two are almost inseparable, the latter often arising from the former. A restructuring of staff is likely to be forced on library managers from the outside as a result of the changing manpower situation and the consequent need to re-examine the use of graduate professional staffs. The second strategy will result from greater standardisation in the use of bibliographic records.

Staffing for reader services
Although a recent handbook on professional and non-professional duties was described as a 'working document' for guidance, one reviewer considered that it raised more questions than it answered. There are two points which do however have some bearing on staffing for reader services and organising technical services. First, the professional duties of those involved with reader services are, as described in the book, so numerous that one cannot imagine a professional librarian finding time to do those tasks which normally fall into the category 'other', the usual synonym for book ordering, shelving and a range of other duties. The book puts great emphasis on the need for tasks carried out by junior or clerical staff

to be performed 'under direction' or 'close supervision' of, or 'referred to' a professional but, although one must acknowledge the importance of professional guidance in libraries, junior staff must surely be very unintelligent if they cannot be allowed to execute unattended most of the clerical tasks in libraries. It does not augur well for the effectiveness of graduate professional librarians and the efficiency of reader service areas they operate if they fail to realise the full potential of their junior staff.

For some time now there has been dissatisfaction among library school students with their job prospects. This dissatisfaction is not only that of the student of the non-graduate professional course, who fears his job prospects are receding with the growing influx of graduates into the profession, but also of graduates. Both are disillusioned by the prospect of doing the kind of work they have experienced, not only in unqualified pre-library school work situations but also during their practical work as library school students. They suspect that they will end up doing the same soul-destroying jobs such as preparing or 'supervising' binding, looking after reading rooms in which they have no real interest, on evening duty, or simply doing 'clerical, routine, undemanding' work. Beyond the library school—an institution which tends to bring out the pessimistic side of library students anyway—this is in fact very often the situation. Fred Bungay's research into first post appointments showed those involved to have a high level of anxiety and frustration, a state of mind which began during the period of professional studies and which was not alleviated during the first year of professional activity.

Sergean and McKay have rightly stressed that 'selection is not always just a once and for all matter of filling an applicant into a slot, but of fitting him or her into an organisation with future changes in mind'. A major cause of the lack of planned development and failure to remember these future changes is the absence of any adequate job description to help the manager with his selection. A more detailed analysis of what a subject specialist does or how library use instruction forms an essential aspect of reader service would 'seem to make more realistic the expectations of both users and potential recruits'.

Roberts' recent survey showed professional graduate librarians to be dissatisfied with the nature of the work in their first jobs, especially in the area of technical duties and where there was no direct contact with readers. He also stresses the close connection between the level and quality of service provided and job dissatisfaction. It seems strange that although library managers must be aware of this, they do not seem to react to the urgency of the situation. A prerequisite for efficiency in library services is job satisfaction, especially if customer satisfaction is affected by staff satisfaction. Both the CLMRU and the Sheffield surveys confirm that graduates, especially in their first jobs—those jobs where, given the right conditions, the natural enthusiasm of the newly qualified librarian can produce job satisfaction—have, as their principal duties, the traditional specialisations of cataloguing and classification.

Academic libraries seem to depend 'upon the willingness of graduates' to do their mundane technical jobs as well as their cataloguing and classification. Fifteen percent of the Sheffield sample had filing as their principal duty, twelve percent had circulation, whilst six percent had shelving! Although some of this may have been work of a supervisory nature, one wonders if libraries are getting the best out of their graduate professional staff. On the other hand, the complaisant graduate professional attitude of 'expecting to do the donkey work' does not augur well for their expectations of achieving early responsibility in the reader service areas. Weber and Rogers have stressed that some posts do exist which exploit individual talents rather than fitting people into 'rigorously defined jobs'. This trend in job placement continues, in the findings of the Sheffield survey, into second posts with 'classification maintaining a pre-eminent position as the principal duty, partly because of its association . . . with subject specialisation and subject knowledge' and partly, perhaps, because it falls less easily into the processing chain of acquisitions-cataloguing-classification, which tend to be associated with centralised processing units.

Library managers can help to overcome the cause of such dissatisfaction by clearly differentiating between what they want their graduate professional librarians to do and what they wish the rest of their staff to do. This has been demonstrated by Guttsman at the University of East Anglia library who has given his subject specialists a range of administrative tasks such as giving consultative advice and responsibility for general oversight rather than extensive involvement. The situation at East Anglia is similar to that outlined by Woodhead at University College London (UCL), where the subject specialists are also responsible for 'other work'. Woodhead's study re-emphasises the unsatisfactory nature of the work carried out by subject specialists in many academic libraries in the UK which means that they fall between two stools. For, although subject specialists expect their work to include the core areas of book selection, liaison with teaching staff, and library instruction, many of these have to be neglected due to the other demands on their time. This means that the need to 'compromise between functional operations and subject specialisation' is highly unsatisfactory with 'the wide variety of jobs that specialists perform and, in particular, the amount of time spent on routine work such as cataloguing, re-cataloguing, checking, typing and the comparatively small amount of time spent on more creative aspects of subject specialisation work such as assistance to readers'. It would be interesting to see how 'general oversight' works in practice in the University of East Anglia library. Although from experience one might expect a situation not unlike that described by Woodhead at UCL and at Leeds, a grain of optimism may be gleaned from Guttsman's emphasis on 'intellectual astuteness and academic attainment' as the principal qualities of his subject specialists. Any resulting clash with the traditional need for a librarian to develop qualities of 'administrative competence', can partly be avoided by involving members of the subject specialist staff in decisions affecting the library as a whole. Weber and Rogers have emphasised that great encouragement can be given to young professional staff by asking them to participate in the decision-making process. In the development plan of the Wolverhampton polytechnic library, W J Simpson notes how only a 'promising' staff structure, one in which the staff feel they have an effective say in the implementation of reader service policies, can attract an enthusiastic and intelligent graduate professional staff.

Roberts, in the Sheffield survey, re-emphasises that subject specialists are, in fact, both subject and technical specialists because of the variety of ways in which duties are emphasised and because of the differing interpretations of the role of the subject specialist. For example, the previously mentioned problem of classification duties can be seen to have both service and functional significance. Most of the duties performed by any one subject specialist could be interpreted as being within reader service areas and also as having a distinct bias towards the use of subject expertise and knowledge. The automatic inclusion of cataloguing as a principal task for first post-graduate professional employees still seems to be the odd man out in a range of professional duties not necessarily linked to reader services, just as the frequent exclusion of library use instruction as a principal task for reader services might be surprising. However, it may be that the decline of cataloguing as a principal task, will see a corresponding increase in instruction in library use.

This problem of where to place cataloguing as a library task falls within the more general problem of what kinds of work actually constitute librarianship, a question raised by both Guttsman and Thompson. Tasks traditionally regarded as a 'librarian's', namely cataloguing, circulation control, periodicals accessioning, and book ordering, are not jobs belonging to professionalism but to a range of duties more aptly categorised as clerical and which only just qualify 'for even sub-professional supervision; the work itself could be done by monkeys'. Such jobs as labelling, shelving, accessioning are mundane and always will be so. Not only is it odd that we should want to offer such jobs to professionally qualified librarians, but even more peculiar, that people should be willing to accept them. Thompson's analysis list is eventually reduced to a small number of what one can honestly label as graduate professional library tasks and a much larger number labelled back-up clerical staff tasks. Examining the latter, cataloguing, a 'traditional' professional task, is categorised as a clerical task; with the firm establishment of centralised cataloguing as an economy measure, it will become even less demanding and receive its rightful place in the hierarchy of clerical library tasks.

Crossley, in a recent article takes a step in the same direction and refutes the case for including classification as a subject specialist duty in university and polytechnic libraries on the very practical grounds that the subject specialist often winds up spending too much time on this work at the expense of his other duties which were originally meant to take priority. He concedes an advisory capacity for classification duties though this would have to be treated with some caution. Increasingly, the librarian, as manager, is going to have to ensure that the reader service duties which new staff have been promised are guaranteed. In their own minds, these new employees can do without the essential but soul-destroying tasks associated with technical duties. Demanding reader services work compensates for such inconveniences as 'cramped working conditions', another cause of dissatisfaction among newly qualified graduate professional recruits. The absence of satisfactory working conditions can lead to job dissatisfaction but their presence does not necessarily guarantee job motivation. Plate and Stone have found that librarians respond positively to such motivational factors as a sense of achievement, recognition and work that is intrinsically satisfying. The chances of these working conditions occuring in polytechnic libraries are probably greater than in university libraries. Despite this, the reasonableness of enthusiastic, well-motivated staff is such that, given interesting work, they will be prepared to accept other limiting conditions of work.

Exploring technical services
The split-site legacy of the polytechnic is one which makes great demands on all technical service support staff, clerical or professional, normally at the expense of professional reader service tasks.

Woodhead quotes Fern's observation in the latter's study of the libraries of the new universities, that 'subject specialisation tends to work at the expense of efficiency in technical processes'. If efficiency in technical processes is a euphemism for a reduction in local cataloguing and the reliance on centralised services, then this author for one would feel that such a decline is not wholly without benefit. Moreover, this seems to have been the solution favoured by several of the UCL and Leeds subject specialists interviewed by Woodhead. If the detailed breakdowns of the times spent by the subject specialists on their subject work are at all accurate, where such tasks as cataloguing, checking cataloguing, binding, transmitting orders and 'other things' seem to predominate, then the remedy referred to above by Fern, albeit unwillingly, will go a long way towards solving a frustrating situation. In the Wolverhampton development project, Simpson notes that two years after the plan's publication the library had not made much headway in reader services because of the 'backlog of unordered, uncatalogued and unprocessed books' which resulted in a concentration of resources on the basic tasks of processing materials.

An easy solution is that of increasing the number of clerical support staff either by a redefinition of tasks or simply by an increase in the clerical staffing establishment. Both are generally difficult to accomplish. Bloomfield's memorandum to the Committee on Library Resources of the University of London suggested that because no savings can be made in the future on administrative costs, and because readers are asking for extra services, there seems to be room for economies only in the areas of acquisition and processing of materials.

Centralisation of technical processing is a positive response to a need and one which, if it is remembered that it is only a means to an end, can be relied upon to avoid conflicting with the demands of reader services. Half measures are no use; if flexibility is allowed so that local practice is given priority over other considerations then the potential gains of centralised technical services will be seriously limited. Richard Dougherty quotes David Kaser as asserting that most of the reasons for the failure to cooperate, for example, in the areas of cataloguing and classification, are psychological and sociological—'long standing local traditions and practices can produce serious interlibrary incompatibilities' and the more cooperation 'affects a library's local policies and procedures the less the likelihood' that cooperation will be received with enthusiasm. Procedural compatability depends to a large degree for its effectiveness on the impact of standardisation on bibliographic uniformity. This can be examined by looking at the use of MARC data; and the willingness to accept standardised book processing.

A constant source of wonder in academic libraries is the way technical services have maintained their ascendancy over other services often at the expense of the user. An illustration of this is the way in which, especially in a decentralised system, the need for standardisation of procedures has been resisted. How long this can, or should, continue in a period of increasing uniformity is a moot point. Coward has noted that one of the principles on which BNB MARC is based is the necessity to 'accept satisfactory standards where they exist and adopt new standards when they are prepared'. It is BNB's responsibility to offer these standards and it is the library's responsibility to accept them—as a duty to their users if for no other reason.

Whatever the source or type of cataloguing used, whatever the system of overall processing used, the academic library functions primarily as an information store; users want information on the spot, not a reference to information elsewhere. This may be an oversimplification of a situation but it is one which applies in polytechnic libraries. The catalogue is the largest and most direct method for displaying a library's materials. Neither catalogues nor classification schemes have been as successful in living up to their maker's intentions or their user's aspirations as the efforts and resources put into them warrant. The few recently published surveys on undergraduate use of catalogues in academic libraries bear this out. McLean maintains that the catalogue is used largely to find the location of books on the shelves rather than to find further bibliographical information on particular materials. Maltby and Sweeney's UK survey emphasised very little use of descriptive details; they go so far as to indicate that 'much of the latter does not justify its existence in the cataloguing record'.

When one begins to examine the possible reasons for such failures we are tempted to assume that more effort in such reader service areas as library use instruction, at the expense of the efforts put into local descriptive cataloguing, might help to alleviate such failures. The failures at Cambridge and Leicester University libraries described in SC33 (a)–(d) by CLMRU resulted in the main from inadequate references from lecturers or from inadequate reading lists. Both surveys hint at a lack of liaison between library and teaching staff, and a failure to help teaching staff to appreciate the importance of sound bibliographical references for reading lists, and also the need to implement an effective library instruction programme. Observation of the reactions of those who have failed at the catalogue may be a useful guide to librarians intending to improve reader services. It is possible that better advice and improved reader instruction on the use of a simplified catalogue would represent a better investment than the traditional approach to library cataloguing. Whatever the reasons for the failures of reader services to satisfy their user's need either at the catalogue or at the shelf, a greater allocation of staff resources, in time and numbers, to instruction programmes and to liaison with academics can only be achieved in a split-site situation by centralising on other resources.

Several polytechnic libraries have begun to establish central processing services. Both Liverpool and Central London Polytechnic libraries have opened such units and it is expected that they will progress from this to acquisitions and cataloguing operations. Weber and Rogers' remark that 'it actually makes not a great deal of difference whether a beginning is made in acquisitions or cataloguing since the library should base its efforts on the MARC record in either event and will have to do preliminary work on both acquisitions and cataloguing before doing detailed system design on either one'. Coward has also stressed that MARC, though designed as a cataloguing service, cannot be entirely separated from other administrative operations, particularly those associated with acquisitions work.

The only published detailed analysis for the planning of a polytechnic centralised processing unit is that done by the City of London Polytechnic library (Pritchard and Auckland) whose objective was to analyse current procedures in use, for the sub-areas of selection, bibliographic checking, ordering, receipt, accessioning, cataloguing and physical processing. By observing norms of time, output and cost, it was possible to calculate costs and effectively regrade tasks or combine standard elements to perform the same function. The COLP Book Ordering and Processing Survey revealed scope for simplification and change, reducing the cost of book processing and producing a faster flow of books through the system. The amount of time spent on routine and bibliographic checking, as well as the existence of four different classification schemes and differing catalogue records, was also seen to be wasteful of professional staff time. The final recommendations were to promote unified practices among the various sites, and to simplify and improve bookflow. Bibliographic checking was to be done by trained junior staff and centralised cataloguing would be brought in to reduce the pressure on staff whose work would then essentially consist of classifying and cataloguing non-BNB items. This survey also stressed the need to standardise on one cataloguing code (1967 AACR) and one classification scheme (18th DDC). A major difference between a centralised acquisitions system for a cooperative which the libraries of the University of London would represent and a split-site polytechnic library such as the City of London Polytechnic, lies in the area of duplication. The Committee on Library Resources (CLR) of the University of London recorded little duplication in their survey although multiple copies of important monographs were common. The level of duplication in the University of London libraries did not exceed the level of necessity. Urquhart and Schofield noted that the 'degree of duplication between orders with personal authors is much higher than between orders which are recorded by title only . . . The most reasonable explanation for this effect is that orders with no personal authors are more likely to apply to specialised documents collected by one library only'. One could also reasonably add that such specialised documents collected by a specialised library, were the result of a greater emphasis on research collections in institutions such as the University of London libraries. At this stage in the development of the polytechnic libraries, the percentage of duplicated materials, mainly for undergraduate use, and presumably of personal author BNB materials, would probably be much higher; furthermore, the split-site library demands a level of necessary duplication for such common materials as catalogues, bibliographies, guides and other common forms of reference works. W Ashworth has pointed out that 'no quantitive study has yet been made of the extra cost of multi-site libraries'. He remarks that the rough estimates which have been made so far, not less than five percent per site 'that is to say, for two sites one would add ten percent, for three fifteen percent and so on . . .' are estimates which cover materials and staff. Certainly the polytechnic libraries are acquiring material which is undergraduate in the nature of its use, and which is generally found in BNB and LC MARC. COLP's study noted that sixty seven percent of all their titles received were in BNB, whilst a small survey from the Polytechnic of North London found sixty four percent.

 The freeing of graduate, professional staffs from routine matters implies that certain technical operations would be manned by clerical staff with perhaps a non-professional senior assistant acting as supervisor. Such assistants might include students or other part-time help. Similarly with cataloguing. Intelligent library assistants can develop 'professional cataloguing' skills. People who can follow rules, have a capacity for accuracy and bibliographical skills, are not difficult to find provided that training and motivation are readily available.

Before we finish with central processing, it is worth mentioning the significance of classification in the central processing chain. In terms of subject analysis, it would still be regarded as not only a 'professional' library task but one which fits into the mainstream of subject work for the graduate professional librarian in the reader service area. As already mentioned, Crossley comes nearest, in the many recent papers on subject specialisation in the academic library, to advocating the abandoning of classification from the subject specialist's work because of the danger that he will become immersed in routine work. He adds the proviso, however, that there might be a place for an advisory capacity in classification duties without it being taken to the limit. To some extent, the problem of where to place classification depends on whether it should be regarded merely as a tool for broad subject arrangement with the catalogue assisting in specific searching, or whether it should be used to introduce specific classification. Needham states that a 'fair degree of specific classification is needed for satisfactory browsing', and that browsing is a significant and important part of intellectual development. This latter judgement may be true, but, in practice, only greater emphasis on it by reader services will promote browsing from being an insignificant part of the undergraduate user's behaviour in the polytechnic library to being 'an important part of intellectual development'. Maltby and Sweeney's survey emphasised that users of the catalogue were primarily concerned with obtaining a call mark and finding that call mark on the shelf. The COLP study on the length of DDC 18 class numbers opted for specificity rather than brevity, although they were not sure of the extent to which users do not find a book because of the length of specific class numbers, nor indeed how far users neglected to consult the catalogue in the first instance. However, one feels the COLP advocacy of the inclusion of classification in the centralised processing system is on the grounds of economies of staff time rather than its exclusion for reasons of 'intellectual integrity'.

The moral of centralised processing, says Richard Dougherty, is to accept the processed book as it is received. Public libraries are adept at doing this. The degree of effectiveness of technical processing centres to their member libraries is directly related to the degree that the member library is willing to accept the cataloguing and classification as it stands. It would take a strong cataloguing nerve to accept all this. In practice, it might not be necessary. The Ohio College Library Centre permits libraries to receive catalogue cards edited to satisfy local idiosyncracies. In the same way, Ayres, as long ago as 1971, remarked that MARC will become viable when 'we have devised methods at the local level which are able to integrate the records that we require from MARC into our own systems'. In effect, this is what is happening in the BRIMARC scheme, with libraries able to obtain a MARC tape tailor-made to cover their requirements.

Despite what has been said above, the nature and definition of reader services in academic libraries is still very much open to interpretation. What is increasingly evident is a restriction on resources accompanied by pressure for more effective utilisation of such resources. Wherever the emphasis on library services, whether it be reader services or not, there is no doubt that a proper groundwork must be laid for the effective on-going operation of the library. Only when this has been accomplished, can one progress to the 'luxuries' of reader services. Adequate back-up facilities in the form of clerical staffing support, and an ability to recognise and act upon growing technical development in library processing must be present. The recent establishment of polytechnic libraries, alongside contemporary technical developments has given reader services a chance to establish a stronger foothold in the priority of things and it is hoped that such an opportunity will not be wasted. However, this will depend on the achieving of a proper balance between sound technical support services and the more exploitative aspects of the professional librarians' duties.

CHAPTER III

Public relations and publicity

Denis Heathcote

PUBLICATIONS AND PUBLICITY are but aspects of public relations, itself only one method of the promotion of library use. Public relations cannot be considered in isolation from library services or instruction in library use. The provision of an efficient service acts as a considerable means of promotion in itself, but to suppose that it is all that one needs to do is too simplistic. There has been some reaction, particularly in the United States, against library publicity on the grounds that it is absurd to promote library services as if they were consumer goods, but this is to view public relations as if it consisted of nothing but the grosser manifestations of the PR man's skills. The techniques of erotic illustration however irrelevant to the product, or promotional competitions, or trading stamps, are not what I am concerned with. Nor am I advocating selling the library short by pretending it is something it is not. Academic libraries provide information services not amusement facilities.

Greta Renborg, writing of public relations activities of the Stockholm City Library, defined them in this way. 'The primary purpose of public relations is to create and maintain good relationships with individuals and groups inside and outside the organisation . . . as an overall concept, it is one part of the total activity of the organisation'. This is far removed from the business of instilling an image which is deliberately or accidentally divorced from reality. Public relations for libraries involves making users or potential users aware of exactly what a library is and what services it can provide for those who need them. Librarians need no convincing that they provide services relevant to the needs of their users, but it does sometimes seem difficult to persuade the users that they have needs that can be met by a library.

Perhaps it is the slenderness of polytechnic library resources, when compared with most British university libraries, that has led polytechnic librarians to place particular emphasis on the fullest possible exploitation of their stocks. The origins of the polytechnics in mergers of technical colleges, colleges of commerce and education, and other institutions which generally had small and underfinanced libraries, has meant that polytechnic libraries have had to work hard to measure up to the standards required by a rapid expansion of degree courses, and to establish the value and relevance of library services. The scale and ratio of expenditure on materials and staff allowed by the Inner London Education Authority have made possible both the development of subject specialist services and concentration on encouraging the fullest use of library resources, in the Polytechnic of North London. Other polytechnics with less generous finances and establishments have similar beliefs and intentions but are not always in a position to advance at the same speed.

Why public relations?

One hardly needs to look for signs that libraries and librarians enjoy a poor image, not helped by the media. Indeed, the signs force themselves upon one's attention from all quarters. At least, 'the mainstay of the public library' by courtesy of Smirnoff Vodka, was pretty, whereas the mass media seem determined to perpetuate the hoary myths of libraries as dusty and old fashioned, and librarians as dull and eccentric. Other commentators sometimes distinguish the helpfulness of the librarians but contrast this unfavourably with the difficulties of understanding and finding one's way around libraries. A humorous feature article in the *Sunday times* in July 1973 made just this point, remarking unfavourably on the lack of use of catalogues in public libraries and the omission of promotion and explanation of their use.

These examples show the extent to which libraries and librarians may be misunderstood in general, but are we justified in thinking the situation in institutions of higher education is any more satisfactory? While in purely quantitative terms, academic libraries may have a more committed clientele, there is evidence to suggest that all is not well. Though all academic librarians are probably aware of several senior, respected teaching colleagues who appear able to ignore and, in some cases, be hostile to library services, any survey evidence seems to be lacking. Evidence for student attitudes to books and libraries has been collected by Peter Mann at Sheffield University and published in a number of forms. He has found that rather large proportions of students make little or no use of university library facilities, though the existence of departmental libraries detracts somewhat from the force of the figures. Even though many students used the university library as a study facility, not using the library stock, some fifteen percent did not even use it for this purpose and among students of applied science, the percentage rose as high as twenty five percent of those sampled. About twelve percent of all students sampled spent no time at all in the university library in a typical week, and again much higher percentages of non-users were to be found among students of science and technology. As many as half those surveyed who were studying law, pure science and medicine, had no books at all on loan from the university library. Even among students of the humanities whose library use is demonstrably and understandably heavier than most, there were small but significant proportions who made no use of the university library. Comments by students on library services, revealed some constructive suggestions but also a frequent lack of appreciation of what services were provided. Even when questioned on which libraries they used for study purposes, many admitted they used no library at all; about a quarter of the sample studying architecture, engineering and materials technology, and nearly twenty percent of those studying medicine and pure science.

If this situation can be said to be typical of British higher education institutions, then clearly there is work to be done on improving services and publicising them. In the Polytechnic of North London library service, there are crude indications of a degree of non-use. Of fourteen hundred students registered as library users on enrolment day in one building in autumn 1973, about three hundred had not claimed their full allocation of four tickets by Easter 1974, and many had not materialised at all. Granted that there are other factors involved, dropping out from courses for one, this shortfall cannot be ignored. The library involved is that containing principally architecture, science and technology collections. The experience of my colleagues who undertake instruction in library use is frequently that of encountering ignorance of what any library has to offer or of how to use its services.

It is necessary, in my opinion, to promote the fullest use of the resources and services provided for polytechnic students, teaching staff, research staff, and administrative staff. Not only is there scope for improvement in services to students, but also, there is a clear need to persuade some teaching staff that an academic library can offer more than just the book repository function. In addition to the long accepted library functions, service oriented librarians are developing a range of services, often based upon a subject specialist team, such as information services, instruction in library use and in bibliographical techniques, and current awareness services for new publications. This extension of services is not always accepted gratefully; it can engender suspicion if not hostility from some academics who see in it a threat to their own professional expertise. On the other hand, librarians wish to persuade their users not only of their ability to undertake such activities but of their undoubted right to do so. There is at least one polytechnic in which the library's role is so underdeveloped, that it does not control, let alone, initiate the bulk of expenditure on library materials. The bookfund is split among a number of teaching departments, leaving the librarian an amount for reference books and general material. Nor do academic librarians agree on the extent to which the provision of services by subject specialist librarians should go. Charles Crossley in a recent paper, discusses just this point, and points out what is considered to be desirable at Bradford University, stops short of what polytechnic authors (Holbrook, Harris), have advocated. It also falls short of the standard at which the Polytechnic of North London library service is aiming.

The means of public relations

Provision of a really excellent service is, no doubt, one of the most effective means of promotion of use, but it does suffer from the inevitable drawback of preaching to the converted and relying on recommendation by word of mouth. As a long term strategy, this may be effective for the relatively stable clientele of academic teaching staff, but it will hardly be enough to affect student attitudes. Nevertheless, the provision of services in depth to polytechnic teaching departments, does seem to be valued by the recipients and to create intensified demand for library service. Apart from its promotional value, provision of a library service forms the foundation for extension of service activities.

The policy for public relations is summarised by the title of a once popular song, 'Accentuate the positive, eliminate the negative'. Placing emphasis on the strong points of a library service, while working to improve weakness, is not necessarily to gloss over failings. Polytechnic libraries, often hampered by split site working, embarrassed by too few staff and too many service points, and sometimes still suffering from the effects of amalgamation and merger, may be involved in painful and wearisome struggles to eliminate the negative aspects whether human or material.

Failure to maintain efficient library routines, such as circulation systems, periodical files, or interlibrary loan systems, offends users to an extent out of proportion to their significance to librarians. Only one failure in a hundred may seem very creditable to us, but to the recipient of a misplaced overdue letter, or to the lecturer whose request arrives two months after it was required without a word of explanation, it will appear in an altogether different light. Librarians publicly claim to be organisers and retrievers of information, but some libraries, with low standards of tidiness and orderliness give a different impression. Although library accommodation in polytechnics is frequently not what one would like, failure to provide readily perceptible layouts and clear guiding is inexcusable.

Staff behaviour is most important in influencing users. Poor performance can only serve to accentuate an already poor image. Not all librarians possess outgoing natures and motivation to serve users, but must be educated to regard them not as interruptions but as people. The aim should be to give the enquirer the feeling that answering his problem or enquiry is the librarian's most pressing concern, while maintaining a proper sense of priorities about the immediate tasks and more regular duties. Peter Jordan has described how a library atmosphere has as much to do with staff behaviour as with the physical surroundings. It seems more than likely that users take their cue from staff and regulate their behaviour accordingly. This is clearly shown in the matter of noise in the library. Without enforcing absolute silence, a quiet atmosphere, conducive to study, is desirable in academic libraries, but Peter Jordan cites examples where staff noise was felt by users to hinder them in the pursuit of their studies. Courtesy to users, even under provocation, is another *sine qua non* for good public relations and it need not be at the expense of informality. It is all too easy for members of library staff, when faced for the umpteenth time that day with a reader who prefers to ask rather than use the catalogue, to succumb to the temptation of adopting an unhelpful attitude. Many people unwittingly affect an unhelpful telephone manner quite at variance with their usual selves. Once again, in public relations terms, this could be disastrous and it certainly detracts from the service oriented library. On every occasion when a librarian, professional and non-professional, makes contact with a user, it should be the librarian's concern to make it clear that he or she is offering a service, is trying to help meet a particular need. Let me immediately add, however, that adopting this attitude does not necessitate giving in to the occasional library pest, it simply means being courteous while disposing of the problem.

Improvement of librarian to user personal contacts should be possible by training, particularly if we can record or videotape actual confrontations, but trying to inculcate a more helpful attitude to users in this way is superficial. Motivation is the key and to motivate junior professional and non-professional staff, the senior librarians must lead by example.

One last point regarding improvement of contact between librarian and user concerns anonymity. Extension of services by subject specialist librarians and encouragement of close liaison with academic staff is not to my mind compatible with professional anonymity. Stimulating better professional relationships necessitates both parties knowing who is who. In the High Street war for custom conducted by the banks, identification of counter clerks was an early development. Let us at least make it apparent to users whether they are talking to a junior assistant or senior professional by labelling either our desks or even ourselves.

Even though librarians need to pay attention to establishing a more helpful attitude to users, it is in the printed form of notices, standard forms and letters, that we often let ourselves down. In the desire to be brief and to the point, too often a peremptory tone may creep in, which is naturally resented and all the more so if, for example, a borrower is being commanded to return a book which he has already returned. Too many prohibitory notices about the library may unintentionally present an impression of authoritarianism which is likely to be at variance with what the present generation of students expect and many librarians are trying to convey. Nor is there any evidence from the five libraries at the Polytechnic of North London that behaviour is in any way affected by the presence or absence of admonitory notices such as NO SMOKING. What is apparent is that users regulate their behaviour by reference to the prevailing standards. Some service points rarely have to ask smokers to desist, some have a continuing problem.

In promoting their services, academic libraries are not competing with manufacturers of consumer goods, but they exist in an environment in which certain ideas and methods of publicity are current. The generally accepted conceptions of what constitutes efficiency or popular appeal of service organisations cannot be totally ignored. There is an element of self-fulfilment here of course, but without trying to turn libraries into imitation supermarkets, one can derive useful pointers from their practice. In this respect at least, libraries are competing with the promotional activities of other organisations, in competition to gain attention, in order to communicate.

I do not believe that libraries should be supermarkets, though just a little of their approach may have its uses, or that they should seek to emulate their appearance. But the attributes which shoppers seem to find desirable and with the services provided. Shops which attract custom by making available a wide range of goods, have to do not just with price, but with the range and quality of goods, clearly displayed and open to examination, by adopting clear layouts and adequate guiding, by prompt and courteous attention and service, provided by helpful and informed staff, can and do operate from premises old and new, traditional and modern. Their potential is not necessarily related to frantic attempts to be fashionable and trendy but to the substance of the goods and services they provide. And so it is with libraries. Public relations is not about superficial images, but about the promotion of the substance of library services, which librarians strive to make as valuable to users as possible.

Library printed materials
The range of publications produced by an academic library is competing for attention with promotional material coming from inside and outside the organisation. Teaching staff are inundated with paperwork concerning academic and organisational matters, apart from sales material from commercial organisations. Other service departments, extra mural studies, the language laboratory, the media and educational technology, are all hard at work promoting their services. Students are similarly afflicted by course material, handouts, reading lists, by careers advisory bulletins and student union publications. In this situation, poorly produced library publications will not only fail to make any impact but will also help to reinforce a poor image of the library. Any one individual may have very limited personal contact with library staff and so form his impressions and attitudes towards library services almost entirely on the basis of the literary guide, a poorly worded handout, a sloppily produced bulletin or a tattered notice. His initial contact with the library may be in the printed form and no amount of helpfulness at the counter will be able to overcome an early bad impression.

Some polytechnic libraries, to judge by their publications, are able to hand over graphic design to a professional on the staff of the in-house reprographic unit, others equally as clearly are unable or choose not to exercise this option. To make a senior librarian responsible for all public relations and publications is a luxury to which most staff establishments will not stretch. Nevertheless, given a little consideration, some academic institutions achieve striking and handsome results, using nothing more than library typists and the ability to use transfer lettering systems effectively.

Critical consideration of the graphic design standards of library publications seems to be rare, indeed only one has been brought to my attention, and it relates to Canadian public library publications. Despite that, the judgements could apply to much academic library printed material. Leslie Smart castigates the weakness of illustrations, the use of discordant typefaces, poor photographic standards, the prevalence of stabbing as a form of binding, the frequent failure to establish a unified style for all the publications from one library, and the continuing adherence to the use of heraldic devices. With regard to library publications produced in-house, I would add low standards of typography and reproduction.

Let me be clear. I am not advocating that all library printed material be professionally typeset and printed, with half tones and line illustrations. Each publication should be produced in a manner and by methods consistent with its purpose. Some may justify letterpress printing, by virtue of quantity and quality required, many will be more appropriately produced on small offset machines either in a captive print unit or commercially. Plates will be produced on a typewriter or by other cold composition methods. Whatever the level of sophistication, the means of production must match the contents of the publication. It would be as absurd to produce current awareness bulletins by letterpress, as it would to use a stencil duplicator to reproduce a library guide intended for the whole student body of a polytechnic.

Librarians who are concerned with publications probably are aware of the benefits of establishing close and friendly relations with the staff of their reprographic and printing units. Once they know exactly what its technical capabilities are, of printing, plate making, binding, and headlining, they will be able to plan publications with a far greater degree of assurance of success. The possibility has to be faced that the investigation will result in deciding to use commercial printers for higher quality or quantity work. The necessity then is the establishment of a realistic budget for library publications, which will cover both internal and external costs. This may require argument with those who control financial affairs inside and outside the library service.

Before discussing academic library guides, I must confess to a certain hesitancy. Both in designing publications for the Polytechnic library service and in discussing those of other institutions, I am wary of elevating my standards of taste to become a reference point against which to make value judgements. However, our decision to work towards a unified or family style for our library publications has somewhat lessened the occasion of possible conflict among colleagues.

Library guides

I propose to deal at some length with printed guides to the library, because they seem to be an almost universal feature of academic library publication programmes, and because they enjoy the widest circulation among staff and students in their universities or colleges. I have been fortunate to have at my disposal, apart from my own files, the large collection of library guides at the Polytechnic of North London School of Librarianship, which includes many examples from American universities and colleges.

Guides should not really be judged in isolation, in that they represent only one aspect of promotion of library use. The extent and depth of methods of library instruction whether classroom or media based will, naturally, affect the nature of a printed guide. To pass judgement on a particular guide without being aware of the circumstances from which it arose is also misleading, but as there is no way of knowing whether a particular specimen represents a deliberate compromise between the ideal and expense, or time available for preparation, or restriction to in-house printing, they must be taken as they are found. Moreover, guides may be intended for rather different ends, either to produce a reference handbook covering every aspect of use of a large and complex library, or to provide just enough information to allow the new user to use the basic library services and to give him some idea of what else is available when and if he needs it.

Any examination immediately reveals the obvious: there is no one way, no single formula for an effective guide. There is great variety of approach, reflecting the resources employed in production, the will to communicate, and appreciation of how to do it. The contents may be slight or extensive; often general in nature, guides are sometimes intended for specific user groups, notably students. Polytechnic library guides, compared with those from British universities, certainly lend credence to the idea that one valid difference between the two sectors of the 'binary system' of higher education is that polytechnics tend to be more student oriented than some universities.

Perhaps it is the size and complexity of the older university libraries which makes their guides necessarily rather factually inclined, with much detail on a wide variety of matters: the opening hours of each section, the restrictions in use of special collections; details of classification and so on, and always the rules and regulations, usually including a recitation of the penalties enacted by the senate for transgression. The amount of information packed in is not necessarily reflected in the size of the guide, except perhaps in inverse proportion here and there, as in the case of the Universities of London and Cambridge whose guides are miniature pocketbooks of less than A6 format, conventionally printed in formal style. A similar American model, that of Yale Library, attempts to render this bleak approach more palatable by the combination of formal, factual contents, with a gothic cover illustration, gothic type captions and photographs printed without margins. This uneasy alliance of the graphical conventions of several centuries presents a rather bizarre appearance. The chief failing though of this approach is its unreadability. The size and style marks it out clearly as a pocket-reference book for large library collections and this is quite valid, but as a guide for new users, it is almost useless. There is no visual appeal and the arrangement and style in which it is written do not encourage the reader to find out what is on offer.

But it is not necessary to be trendy to be readable and informative, quite the reverse. The American practice of endowing academic libraries and building them to high architectural standards leads many American universities and colleges to produce guides which are almost celebrations of the new buildings, containing much architectural detail. This can lead to somewhat pretentious statements, the relevance of which to a library user is difficult to perceive. Thus, the University of Chicago Joseph Regenstein Library has produced an attractively designed leaflet which unfolds to reveal information on the exterior and interior of the $20M building, but which makes reference in the text to 'the use of the Breuer sled chair in the Thonet version'. Is it nothing but envy that makes me feel this is overdoing things?

Hatfield Polytechnic Library's *Guide for visitors* is a good example of a similar approach that avoids any degree of pretentiousness. But this formal, factual style seems to me to be designed for the user who already knows his way around a library system, who is familiar with catalogues and how to use them, and realises what class marks and call numbers are. Polytechnic experience of new students does not seem to put them into this category. Something much more basic seems to be indicated by the response to library instruction programmes. Some British universities certainly recognise this. *Know your library*, published by the University of Bradford contains a detailed exposition of the catalogue with plentiful examples yet manages to make the whole booklet visually attractive. The Library of York University has produced a single sheet, folded-card, leaflet, which manages to include in its six 'pages', each one third of A4 in size, a photograph of the interior of the library, three floor plans, an outline of the classification, brief information about other libraries in York, hours of opening, how to find a book through the catalogue and how to borrow books, together with several small humorous sketches. All this without, in my opinion, looking overcrowded, indeed even quite stylishly and certainly attractively. It is a leaflet which engages the attention. Just as important as the information content, is the style of its presentation. It tells a student just as much as is needed to use the library's basic services and does it not too formally. Its written style is clear and direct and presents an image of itself as a user-oriented library. This may seem rather thin stuff, but consideration of some glaring examples of the other approach show just how unusual and refreshing this leaflet is.

It is only too easy to find examples which show that the lavish use of paper need not contribute to effective communication. Examples tend to be American if only because British guides are usually low budget publications. The most extreme I have encountered is from the University of Texas, Dental Branch at Houston, whose twenty eight page library resources guide includes eight blank sheets and seven with what appear to be the same floor plan. One of these plans bears no captions at all while the others highlight different areas of one floor. Or is it seven floors? Those quarto-size pages which do contain text are dominated by a heavy sans-serif face. The overall effect is not one of clarity and efficiency but of conspicuous wastefulness.

In contrast to the communication of little information at great length, one can fall into another trap; that of trying to say too much. One British business school included a nine page exposition of the London Business School classification, including explanations of facet analysis and citation order of the facets. Experience at the Polytechnic of North London is that even students of librarianship fight shy of a faceted scheme with a largely alphabetical notation, and I doubt that business school students would have a higher tolerance level.

I have already mentioned that the style of presentation is important, not only for communicating the desired image of the library, but in forming user attitudes. Peter Jordan recently examined factors conditioning behaviour in libraries, one of which it was suggested was possibly the tone and style of printed guides, particularly in a negative

49

fashion by concentration on rules and regulations. My experience suggests that academic libraries are particularly at fault in this respect. Jordan noted that Hull University's library guide contained seven pages on behaviour regulations. Polytechnic guides do not seem to fall into this trap, but I suspect that part of the reason is that insufficient time has elapsed for the gradual accretion of a body of regulations. The Polytechnic of North London only introduced an interim disciplinary code for students in autumn 1973, some two and a half years after designation. Without the ultimate sanctions provided by a general code of conduct, any library regulations would rest on no more than the librarian's moral authority. It must be said, however, that the absence of library regulations has not led to any problems beyond the usual degree of acceptance of library practice and standards of behaviour.

Guides like those of Hull and Sheffield Universities, which contain extensive passages of regulations, present a poor image which probably belies their real nature. So many of the matters dealt with seem hardly to need the authority of regulations. It is common to find among them, opening hours, the accessibility of stacks and book stores, the necessity to fill out registration forms and to obey the requirements of the particular issue system. Penalties of varying weights are prescribed for failure to return books at the proper time and so on. American academic library guides tend to play this down, as do British polytechnic guides, often dealing with no more than loan procedures and basic codes of behaviour. This does not prevent the existence of a formal set of regulations, it simply recognises that a library guide is not an appropriate place to publish them. If the purpose of a library guide is to provide basic library information and to convey an impression of service, the presence of numbered rules couched in formal terms, forbidding this and that, is quite inimical to public relations. Some rules one finds are faintly ludicrous in that they forbid a practice somewhat improbable anyway, *eg*, 'No book may be taken out of the United Kingdom without the permission of the librarian'. Accentuating the positive seems to have been forgotten. In a guide for new library users, it makes sense to emphasise not what one may *not* do, but what services one *can* use. The practice followed in Polytechnic of North London library guides is to request users not to smoke, eat, drink or be excessively noisy for reasons of enlightened self-interest. The prohibition on retention of briefcases in the library is explained by reference to the regrettable need for security measures. These points are made in these terms not just because formal rules would lack teeth, but because my colleagues feel that this approach is more effective that prohibitory regulations. Moreover, I feel that this tone suits the informal style of our library guides, which stress the service above all else. The Polytechnic of Central London library guide adopts a similar approach, but detracts a little from the effect by the unfortunate juxtaposition with the recitation of the legal requirements of photocopying:—

'Photocopying—see individual library. Requests must comply with the provisions of the Copyright Act 1965 and the Copyright (Libraries) Regulation (Statutory instrument, 1957, No. 868).

Rules—These are published separately and are available from the library counters. It cannot be emphasized too much that the Library exists to serve all members of PCL and staff will do their utmost to give a friendly and efficient service. Given co-operation and with mutual exercise of courtesy and common sense in the libraries rules will not need overemphasis. It is, for example, in no one's interest to create noise in the reading rooms or to eat or drink while using books.'

Just occasionally, the desire to suggest appropriate modes of behaviour to library users can become a little humorous. The Ohio State University Libraries' *Handbook for undergraduate students*, under the quotation 'Keep decorum' (Shakespeare. Anthony and Cleopatra 1.2.77 (1605)), asks 'that consideration be shown to your fellow library users by keeping your voice low and controlling public displays of affection'. It seems to be solely an undergraduate problem, as the companion *Handbook for faculty and graduate students* omits this particular appeal.

Not withstanding such unintentional lapses, humour is an element singularly lacking among academic library guides. Possibly, it is thought inappropriate to employ a humorous approach in libraries which rejoice in sonorous titles like 'Keeper of Manuscripts', 'Director of Learning Resources', but the reason is more likely to be that librarians fall into the trap of regarding themselves too seriously. Humour in the text is difficult but in the illustrations, it can sustain interest and help to produce an attractive guide. Imperial College, London produced a guide enlivened by the inclusion of several 'Peanuts' strip cartoons from the series related to libraries, a series which all too well revealed some of the stereotype misconceptions. The text of the guide though was written in a formal style, not altogether consistent with the presence of the cartoons.

Illustration

The use of illustrated captions, cartoons, and diagrams is an effective way of sustaining the students' interest as he turns the pages of a library guide

Plate 1: Cover for an A5 booklet to coincide with a 'special event'. Design by John Minnion. Printed in red and khaki on matt cream card.

It is probable that a guide containing plain text, however well designed, will be read only by committed library users, whereas a guide with text interspersed with appropriate and sometimes amusing drawings, will stand a much better chance of a second perusal when he has left the library and is travelling or relaxing in the coffee bar.

Furthermore, such a design does indicate a marked divergence from the approach the student almost certainly expected from the library. Hopefully, he will be pleasantly surprised to discover that the library is not so hidebound and stuffy as he feared, and might begin to think of it as something more than a book repository, particularly if the emphasis in the library guide is on services. Bear in mind that, for most students, this guide will be his first impression of the library if he receives it on enrolment day or the first time he wanders into the library. It may possibly be some days, even weeks, before he receives library instruction lectures or exposure to tape/slide guides.

Weak drawings are worse than useless, only reinforcing the poor image again. The fact that the Polytechnic of North London library guides are heavily dependent on illustration, is due partly to our good fortune in being able to utilise the services of a former library assistant and commercial artist, John Minnion, who has contributed extensively, in cooperation with the full-time staff, to the appearance of the guides (see Plate 2), to other publications, and tape/slide presentations.

Exactly what makes an illustration weak or strong is impossible for me to express, as it must depend on personal taste. The theme must be relevant to the text it accompanies and not be so obscure that the relevance is not immediately apparent. The skill of the artist can result in drawings with strong, clear lines and a sure feeling.

Floor plans

The quality of floor plans frequently lets down the whole library guide. A poor specimen hardly reinforces the image of the library as the

introduction

You will mainly be concerned with the library at Ladbroke House and this guide sets out to describe the types of library material available here and how to find and use these materials. It is, however, only the first step in showing you the library — we hope you will also check the staff list at the beginning of the Guide so that you know which member of the library staff can help with your particular enquiry. Library instruction will be given to groups at appropriate stages of various Courses by the Subject Specialist Librarians but please ask for individual help whenever needed. No matter which Course you are taking the library can play an important part in your studies.

- 3 -

LIBRARY MATERIALS
AND SERVICES

bookstock

Most of the material here is directly related to the Courses studied in this building, therefore we concentrate primarily on building up a good collection on applied social studies, sociology, law, accounting, economics and business topics. We aim to keep pace with the development of new subjects and Courses and to liaise with Departments in selecting relevant publications. The library also stocks a range of general encyclopaedias, dictionaries, atlases, directories and other background reference works. In addition, there is a small fiction and biography collection.

The Polytechnic is designated as a European Documentation Centre, therefore the library automatically receives various publications of the European Communities.

The number of volumes in stock is about 34,000. New books are displayed near the library entrance and lists of additions are issued regularly.

- 4 -

Plate 2: Double page spread of an A5 library guide. Graphic design by John Minnion.

organiser and provider of information. Their design, however, depends on a careful consideration of what one is trying to communicate. Too much detail will make the plan difficult to use and the captions hard to read, too little information and the whole exercise will be pointless. The aim ought to be to produce a plan which a library user can relate to what he sees as he walks about or remembers the library itself.

Some American guides now seem to favour the very detailed floor plans so beloved by those who organise Bürolandschaft or landscaped offices. In these, the precise location of every stick of furniture is meticulously shown, but the result in a printed guide is far from satisfactory. Such plans suggest a degree of overcrowding by inclusion of such minute detail, and leave little space for inclusion of satisfactorily legible captions. In the large scale form in which originally drawn up, such plans are satisfactory, but reduced to a scale of a few centimetres, the detail becomes disturbing and the captions practically invisible.

Abandoning the use of whatever architectural plans and layouts he may possess, the librarian has to consider drawing his own, or commissioning someone skilled in draughting. I have found it practical to start with a large scale plan, such as that obtained from the building authorities or architects, and to draw on it crudely the main library features; the bookstacks, the periodicals store, staff working areas, the catalogues, information desks, and then to systematically block out superfluous detail, such as columns, and detail within library staff working areas, sometimes even individual bookstacks, until one is left with a simplified plan, containing only those features likely to be necessary for a new user. Choice can then be made of captions for the plan, or on the use of keyed captions, where appropriate, always bearing in mind that they have to be legible at the final size of reproduction.

The three examples reproduced here illustrate these points. They differ not just in that one is clearly amateurish, while the other two are professionally drawn. The first (Plate 3) suffers chiefly from confusion engendered by too many captions, of nondescript appearance. It is difficult to tell where the bookstock on some subjects mentioned is to be found. The actual plan itself has no style, not even differentiating between the boundary walls of the library and internal features, or between internal and external walls. The Hatfield plan (Plate 4) is based directly on the architect's plans, with certain features faded out and others touched up. The economy of detail is excellent but one could maintain that the key numbers are far too large and obtrusive and the captions on the plan itself far too small.

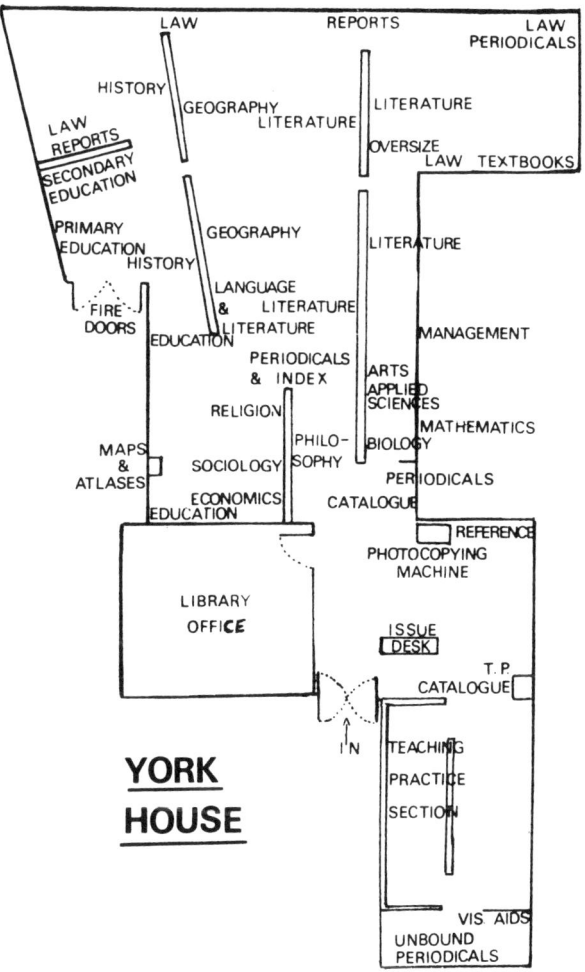

Plate 3: Reproduced with the permission of the copyright holder. Original size 190mm x 120mm.

Second Floor (Technology)

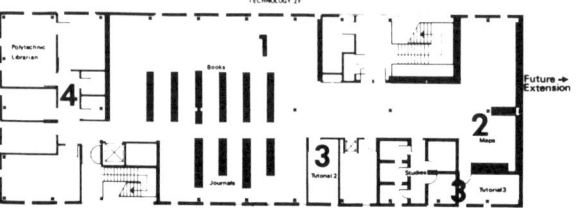

Technology and Engineering (U.D.C. classes 6, 7) books and periodicals for the last six years; also complete holdings of relevant abstracts.

1. Seating area includes special desks, wired to the audio console and equipped with slide projector trays and screens. Designed as multi-media study tables. Microreaders provided in periodicals area.
2. Map and atlas area. Maps are housed in vertical suspension cabinets.
3. Two tutorial rooms and five sound-proof study rooms, all wired to the audio console in the room between.
4. Office suite for County Technical Librarian, his deputy and assistant, and general secretarial office.

Note: Entire wall of the building at the right-hand end is a temporary one, allowing for phase 2 extension.

Plate 4: Reproduced with the permission of the librarian, Hatfield Polytechnic. Original size 140mm x 140mm.

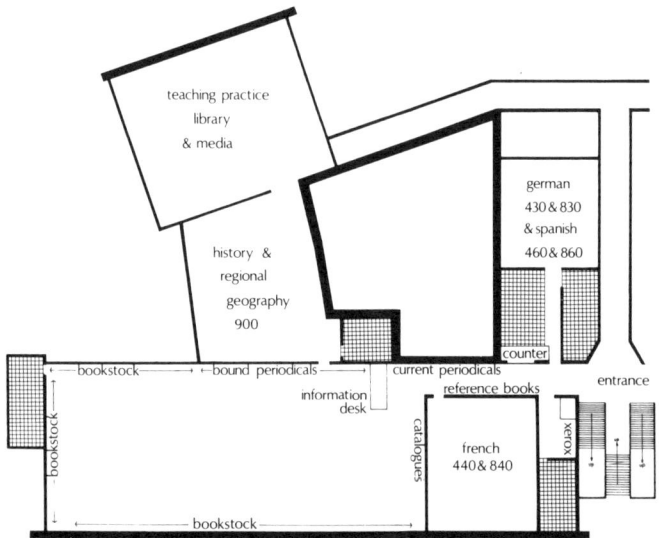

Plate 5: Floor plan of Kentish Town library, Polytechnic of North London. Original size 190mm x 150mm.

The third example (Plate 5) is one designed and executed at the Polytechnic of North London, combining the elements which I and the site librarian agreed to emphasise. The odd shape of the library and its location made it desirable to include some external features, such as the main staircase and adjacent passage ways. As these are main routes in this building, their inclusion here immediately locates the library for the user. The existence of annexes and the two language rooms and consequent splitting of stock, meant that some indication of subjects was necessary. The absence of indication of the bookcases is quite deliberate as their inclusion would have made the captions very cramped, and it was felt that including them added little useful information. Here again, the plan has been professionally drawn by the graphic mainstay of the Polytechnic of North London Library Service publications, John Minnion.

Lastly, what does one do if there is no graphic designer and draughtsman available? Even without any flair for draughting, one can plan carefully what one wants to include, and using building plans, draw up a large-scale library plan, using marker pens, fibre pens and broad nibbed indian ink pens and lettering transfer systems. Reduced photographically either by xerography or the litho plate maker, one can achieve surprisingly good results. The larger one draws the original, the greater the reduction in the scale of imperfections, and the better the result, provided the planning is right.

Production of Polytechnic of North London guides

Most low budget publications seem to be either typed and then produced by one of the duplicating processes or, more commonly, by offset lithography. In either case, typing of high quality is difficult to achieve despite the availability of typewriters with interchangeable typefaces, proportional spacing, and carbon ribbons to give a sharp clear impression. The problem is not so much in this respect but in getting from a typist a product which follows the prescribed layout sufficiently accurately. Following unfortunate experiences, involving typing the same text three or four times, to achieve what I wanted, coldtype composition from a commercial printer has now been adopted. The advantage is chiefly that the text is set by compositors who instinctively use the normal typographical conventions of indenting, spacing, and are aware of the correct proportions of page layouts. This is not to say that they can dispense with clear copy.

My experience in producing a range of five library guides in two successive years embraces two alternative methods of production. On the first occasion, the text was typed on a variety of typewriters, then chopped up, combined with headings, and roughly paginated. Then, retyped in the new page format, it was combined with illustrations for section headings and captions. This necessitated a partial retyping and repagination. Then a final paste-up of text, captions and illustrations took place; the results were sent to a jobbing printer for litho printing and production of the range of booklets. The printer also printed the covers on card with a high gloss finish, to the same design but with a distinctive colour for each library. The results were not always satisfactory chiefly because the typists had not enough time or knowledge to produce really creditable results, and secondly because the illustrator was not involved early enough in the production sequence.

Consequently, a decision was taken to adopt a more expensive procedure. Text was re-written in consultation with each library, and sent for cold composition in the typeface chosen for the Polytechnic's house style, Century. After checking and correction, the printer sent the top copy for use in the final page paste-up. Meanwhile, working on xerox copies of the galleys, the illustrator and I had decided pagination and layouts, combining the text with captions and headings. Having done this four or five times over, it became clear that there was scope for illustrations of certain size, either to introduce a section or to illustrate a particular heading. Most illustrations were used two or three times, and a few were drawn in two versions to match the spaces available. Thus, the illustrations were integrated with text in terms of page layout, and in terms of relevance. There followed an extensive cut and paste session with the top copy of the text and the photographic reproductions of illustrations and letraset captions. This was carried out using a grid representing a page and its print area, on a light box. The pages were then sent to the printer for litho printing. Covers, in this case, were printed on 'coated board', actually thin card with a slight sheen, in the reverse design, shown here.

It must be admitted that the cost has been high, at least £1,000 in payments to printers, photographic artwork, and design fees, to produce five guides with texts that differ, but have some elements in common, *eg*, sections on other library facilities in the locality, or the chief librarian's foreword, and the illustrations and captions. Each cover has been printed in a different colour but to the same design. A typical opening is included here to show the results. The booklets are A5 format, vary in size from 16 to 22 pages, and quantities printed range from 650 to 1150. We feel the cost, as a proportion of the total bookfund, less than one percent, is well justified in terms of the impact the guides have. And next year, as little text as possible will be reset, and used with the same artwork, to produce new editions, probably with a different cover design. By then, the Polytechnic will have acquired another library, and it will then be policy to revise extensively only two of the guides each year, modifying the others as little as possible.

There is one drawback to all the effort and cost put by some libraries into library guides and it is this. They may represent the librarians' conception of effective communication, but do they actually have the desired effects? Some evaluation of their effectiveness is badly needed. So far, all we have tried is to question the odd individual or group, –but the results seem more polite than realistic.

Let me just sum up my basic conception of a printed guide for a service-oriented library system. It should be written and designed for a specific purpose, to give the new user just as much information as he requires to be able to use the library's standard services that are available. Secondly, it should give him clear indications of the atmosphere of the library, by its tone and style, consequently suggesting a pattern of behaviour in library use. Lastly, I hope to impress just a little with the effort made to inform and interest him, so that he may come to believe that a library is a learning resource not just a place for getting hold of books.

Given this approach, which is certainly common, a variety of sizes and format can be found, all valid and effective. What does seem clear is that, to produce a guide in booklet form with satisfactory standards of printing, cover design and illustration, is likely to cost, particularly if one opts to provide a guide for each service point, rather more than most polytechnics would consider justifiable. Even if blessed with but one library, changes in staff and dispositions almost certainly require annual reprints. This one example reveals a major problem for a service oriented academic library, that is deciding what is a valid division of resources devoted to acquiring stock and to its exploitation.

Given the limited finances available to polytechnic libraries, the great variation of library budgets as a percentage of total polytechnic budgets, and the pressures of bringing often inadequate collections up to realistic levels to gain recognition for new course approval by the CNAA, I can well understand why some institutions prefer a more modest and less expensive approach. Indeed, in that library budgets in the Inner London Education Authority polytechnics are based on a capitation system on student numbers without reference to the number of service points or the research activities carried out by academic staff, and that student numbers are not growing as anticipated, our own policy may, in the long run, have to change. Despite annual increases in the capitation amount to cover inflation, budgets for the Inner London polytechnics may actually shrink, though staff numbers cannot be trimmed except by natural wasteage, thus creating even more severe pressure on book funds. It will then be inevitable that more economical means be considered of producing printed library guides and other publications.

Such a change need not necessarily result in less effective publications, as the products of some polytechnics show. The Polytechnic of Central London produces a library handbook covering all its service points, which steers a careful course between material common to all and that specific to each library. Others, including the City of London Polytechnic, Sheffield Polytechnic and Trent Polytechnic, have chosen to employ folders which can contain a range of single sheets containing information on either a particular service point, special collections, the use of catalogues and so on. This solution enables each student to be presented with a package relevant to his particular course and needs, and should lessen the necessity for frequent reprints. It also offers the advantage of enabling him to file the sheets among his notes.

Other library publications
I have written at some length about printed guides because of their importance in library public relations, but they constitute only one element of academic library publication programmes. The range of other publications is wide, bibliographies, accessions lists, journal contents bulletins, current awareness bulletins, journal holding lists, union catalogues of serials, etc. The considerations for production are different from library guides, but just as clearly condition the nature of the publication. The Polytechnic of North London libraries have chosen to abandon monthly accessions lists, even though formerly produced on a site basis, in favour of a range of current awareness bulletins, incorporating relevant accessions. The argument against regularly produced accessions lists is that they usually transgress the basic desiderata for effective communication. They are too long, containing too much information for easy assimilation if one wants to scan the whole production, and that they inevitably contain much information irrelevant to the needs of any one individual or group. However well arranged, however well divided, guided and indexed, they simply provide too large a meal to digest at a convenient sitting and all too frequently are consigned to the wastepaper basket.

The criticisms made of the accessions lists produced at the Polytechnic of North London have not been entirely stifled by the change to more frequent, usually fortnightly or three-weekly current awareness bulletins, containing journal contents pages and recent accessions. In general, the new pattern seems to be more appreciated by the academic staff, for whom they are primarily designed. Production of these bulletins is largely by means of xerography, because in most cases, the quantities produced are beneath or around the number of copies at which it becomes more economical to use offset lithography. The use of paper supplies is economised by using reduction xerography for journal contents lists, and by printing on both sides of the paper wherever possible. The selection of particular contents pages, highlighting particular items of interest, and the choice of accessions relevant to a particular subject area, would not be possible without the team of subject specialist librarians. Procedures have been evolved for minimising the amount of clerical effort by professional staff in production, so that the main burden of copying, typing, collation and distribution is usually borne by the library clerical staff. At the time of writing, current awareness bulletins of this nature are being produced for about a dozen subject areas, including law, sociology, librarianship, applied social studies, history, philosophy, teaching studies, modern languages and environmental science. This concept has not been extended to pure and applied science, for we are not convinced we can improve on the *Current contents in* . . . series, but accessions lists are divided into more specific areas and produced at a frequency designed to keep the length digestible. As acquisitions are at present decentralised, all these bulletins are based on the accessions for individual service points and whereas this is little problem as regards journals, for which considerable duplication exists, it is a problem for books, particularly in subjects which occur in more than one building. New books relevant to the social sciences can crop up almost anywhere in the system. The bulletins are normally distributed automatically to the teaching staff of the appropriate teaching department, made available to their students, and sent to lecturers from any other part of the polytechnic who have requested them. The extent of distribution outside the department for which a bulletin is primarily intended is probably not as great as it could be, but is gradually increasing. To give a distinctive air to these bulletins of several xeroxed pages, paper or thin card front covers of a distinctive appearance are used. Each site tends to use one design, in a number of variations, but all are intended not to impart any degree of permanence but to differentiate this collection

Plate 6: Current awareness bulletins. A4 paper with purple heading.

of paper from all the others that constantly are sent to lecturers. Some depend on similar designs, but paper of different colour, while one group, reproduced here (Plate 6), employs various designs for the title captions but all are printed on A4 paper with a letterhead style, printed in reverse in a bold purple, a colour repeated in the cover of the printed guide to the same library. The 'purple paper' as it is colloquially known, is also used for other small scale publications emanating from the library, such as notes on the law collection, on government publications or local bookshops. Incidentally, these covers are also the work of John Minnion, designer of this book's dustjacket and illustrator of the Polytechnic of North London printed guides. Mention of this small scale 'family look', which attempts to make any document from this library quite distinctive and easily recognisable, and, one hopes, welcome, leads naturally to polytechnic house styles.

Many polytechnic library publications naturally adopt elements of the house style of their institutions, which in general are not very distinguished, though some are highly distinctive and instantly recognisable such as those of Oxford and Wolverhampton Polytechnics. Over half the polytechnics base their style on the use of Univers which is a very useful typeface in common supply, but which suffers from the usual disadvantage of sans-serif faces when used to set text, accentuated often by cold-type composition, that is the minor irregularities of alignment. These are left undisguised by the softening influence of serifs. Anyway, I have to plead guilty to subscribing to the conventional idea that sans-serif faces for text setting impairs legibility. Nevertheless, the most distinctive feature of polytechnic house style is their reliance upon a logotype, involving initial letters or a symbol, or even the whole name in a distinctive style. Use of these logotypes to form part of the design of one's covers is very common but, unless one is fortunate enough to have some designer at hand, it is very difficult to make the library publications distinctive. Some polytechnic libraries, on the other hand, have preceded these institutions in the use of a logotype as house style.

Library notices and shelf guiding constitute another area which forms part of public relations activities. There really is no excuse for handwritten notices, given the availability of transfer lettering systems, or for typed notices positioned where they will remain unnoticed and unread. A few simple experiments can determine the appropriate size of lettering needed to attract attention and be legible from whatever distance is required. Shelf guiding need not be executed in a medium which involves great labour every time the bookstock is rearranged. There are available movable letter systems which are quite adequate. To neglect these matters is hardly to enhance the library's claim to organise and make available its resources.

The frequency with which union catalogues of periodicals from polytechnic libraries land upon my desk is perhaps a reflection of the split-site problem with which so many are afflicted, but I cannot help feeling that too many lack a clearly defined purpose. The most common pattern seems to be an alphabetical list of titles, indicating frequency of publication, length of run, and location, usually between different service points, sometimes within a single large library. They are usually typed documents, quite lengthy and clearly expensive to produce, but of vague purpose. If they are intended for library users, is it likely that any lecturer or student will browse through a list of anything between 1500 to 2000 titles to discover what the library system contains? Is he not more likely to be interested to see only those titles relevant to his main teaching area, and to note that this particular library holds it? For these reasons, my preference is for subject-based lists, and site holding lists with the briefest of details. The union catalogue of periodicals, much used by interlibrary loans staff, is more an internal document. The accurate indication of broken runs and fragmented holdings which this contains would hardly be relevant for the library user.

Whatever we decide to produce, it should be remembered that library printed materials form possibly the greatest area of influence over the user. It is encumbent on the librarian to plan not just the content of his publications to suit the user's needs, but its packaging and presentation as well.

CHAPTER IV

Non-print media

Ann Aungle

IT IS SAD, but true, to admit that many librarians would prefer that the non-print media did not exist. Are we any less reactionary than that fifteenth century monk who, despite Gutenberg's great invention, claimed that his library was a 'true library', ... a place where 'one will find only handwritten manuscripts, and not any of those machine-made reproductions that some have the audacity to call books'? However, libraries must change, just as they changed from being collections of manuscripts to collections of printed books.

The acceptance of non-print materials is proving to be a slow process, particularly in higher education. Books are respectable vehicles for recording and communicating facts and ideas, and they have had centuries of time to build up their reputation. Non-print materials, such as films, television programmes and gramophone records are comparatively recent inventions and their reputation has been associated with the entertainment industry. Their educational potential has been seriously overlooked. It is not only librarians who have been apathetic about these new media, for educators, too, have shown considerable reluctance to try out alternative teaching and learning resources. Librarians have a unique opportunity to initiate change in this area and to make a positive contribution to their educational institution by actively acquiring these new materials and promoting their use among both teachers and learners.

In discussing non-print media, we come up against a very basic communication problem. Everyone knows what a book or journal is, but what are non-print media? The word media is linked in people's minds with the mass communications industry like newspapers and television. In the world of education, we have to explain that the term embraces a wider range of sound and visual resources such as film, videotape, slide, specimen, microfilm, wallchart, sound tape, and so forth. One satisfactory word to describe this array of materials has not yet been evolved. Current expressions such as media resources, non-books, meta books are rather long winded as well as being inexplicit. The old-fashioned term 'audio-visual aids' is now misleading since the emphasis is on learning resources rather than teaching aids. The introduction of jargon from the world of computers, hardware for equipment, software for materials, does little to clarify the issue. The problem of terminology has no doubt contributed to the lack of interest and understanding felt so far by both teachers and librarians.

Whatever we call these audio and visual materials, they do exist. How involved should librarians become with them? Public libraries committed themselves to acquiring and organising non-print media some time ago. Gramophone record collections are now well established and many libraries have been quick to recognise the potential of alternative and varied resources and have given their young customers the opportunity of playing with and learning from multi-media kits. Some libraries attached to organisations like the BBC and the Architectural Association, have specialised in a particular type of media and provide an excellent service to a varied clientele. But do non-print media belong to the world of the academic library? Norman Clarke puts the case well: 'Each type of material has a unique contribution to make in the educational process. Some materials will be more effective in achieving one teaching or learning objective; others will serve another purpose better. There is no competition among instructional materials. The point is that, in any situation, the distinctive characteristics of each medium should be recognised and all appropriate materials should be used'. (Norman F Clarke 'Library education in an era of media' *Contemporary education* November 1969 This statement embraces the total range of both print and non-print media. The book and videotape share equal status. It is short-sighted to ignore the existence of videotape, and similarly it is foolish to claim that tape has supplanted the book.

Microfilm, so far, is the one medium that has been established in academic libraries. Cost of print materials and lack of storage space has forced librarians to buy back runs of newspapers and journals on fiche or film. The arrival of these micro materials has become accepted for these valid economic reasons, though rather grudgingly, by academic staff. Other media have, on the whole, been seriously overlooked by academic librarians.

Traditionally, non-print media have been used as teaching support material. Thus a lecture on architecture might be illustrated by a show of slides. The emphasis is now changing. The potential of media as learning resources in their own right has now been recognised. This has led to the creation of individual learning packages for students, such as tape/slide presentations or videotapes. The production of these media programmes does not mean that the traditional lecture will disappear. The 'chalk and talk' method of presenting information has its place, but it has dominated the teaching scene for too long. The creation of alternative learning resources for students enables teachers to be free from the strictures of formal instruction and be available to give individual assistance and tutorials. There are other advantages for the student: self-instruction allows him to proceed at his own pace; he can study at a time convenient to himself, free of timetable conflicts; he can repeat programmes for revision purposes; he can also concentrate on weaker subjects. Thus the benefits to be gained are quite wide-ranging.

Where should the student expect to find these resources? The natural centre is the library. As Dr Enright asserts in his paper 'Multi-media in libraries', presented to the Library Advisory Council in 1972: 'The library's interest in non-book media is both logical and inevitable. Despite the formidable difficulties confronting the librarian in organising conventional services and the complexity of problems associated with the organisation of multi-media materials, there are major advantages for the user if the new materials can be organised in close association with what have been called the 'old'.' Books are accepted self-instructional materials. It makes sense to have these resources combined with the newer learning media in one central place.

The amalgamation of print and non-print materials has led to the birth of a new unit, usually called a resource centre or instructional materials centre. Some librarians and educationalists have felt that the word 'library' is no longer adequate to define the scope of resources contained therein. If staff and students are educated to expect all types of resources, be they book or non-book, to be housed in the library, there is no need to adopt new terminology. Besides, the phrase 'resource centre' can be misleading. There can be some confusion as to whether the centre is simply an area of media storage or whether the actual production of materials is carried out too. Consequently, establishments have adopted individual interpretations. The library may incorporate a resources centre, which may or may not be involved in production. At the City of London Polytechnic, for example, both library and production unit are amalgamated under the leadership of the Chief Librarian and Head of Learning Resources. Conversely, the library may be under the umbrella of the resource centre. At Brighton Polytechnic, the library and production unit are controlled by an educational technologist. Other institutions, including the Polytechnic of North London, have allowed the library, as storage centre, and the production section to develop separately, though close collaboration between the two is essential. There seems little justification for the rivalry which has sprung up in some places. The function of the two can be clearly defined. The production unit, often called the Educational Technology department, is concerned with the design, creation and assessment of programmes and materials relating to the various courses being taught. This section is also responsible for the provision and maintenance of equipment throughout the establishment. The technical and managerial skills required for implementing these services are totally different from those of the librarian. Our expertise lies in the organisation of information and materials and in storage and retrieval processes. We are already involved in the selection, acquisition, cataloguing, storage and exploitation of print materials. It is logical to apply these skills in the area of non-print materials too.

Cooperation is the keyword between production unit and storage centre. The situation is eased when the heads of both sections are of equal professional status so they can collaborate not only on an informal basis, but also by working together on committees. Liaison between the two units can exist at all levels, with technicians assisting in the maintenance of library machines, and library staff providing an information service on equipment and materials to them.

To summarise the library's role with regard to media, let me quote from the Library Association's general policy statement on library resource centres in schools, colleges and institutions of higher education, published in March 1973. As an official statement, it gives positive direction to the profession on the policies we should be adopting, and it clarifies our role to the outside world.

1   Libraries have always provided some forms of non-book materials in response to demand . . . Books, duplicated and audio-visual materials

complement and support each other in their contribution to teaching and research, and should be regarded as part of a unified collection.

2 a) i The library resource centre should provide a comprehensive source of learning materials in different formats for use by students. These materials should satisfy curricular, cultural and general educational requirements and be available for use both within and outside the library, for independent private study and for class teaching.

2 a) ii The library resource centre collection should include a store of materials . . . embracing both commercially produced media and materials produced within the institution, as well as exchange media.

2 b) The library resource centre staff should classify and catalogue all learning and teaching materials available within the institution . . . Indexes and catalogues should be readily available in the library resource centre.

2 c) The library resource centre staff should provide and disseminate comprehensive information on new materials and curricular developments to all teaching staff.

2 d) The library resource centre staff should use their knowledge of sources and resources to advise the teaching staff on the availability of materials appropriate to their teaching needs . . .

2 e) The librarian should provide help and instruction in the use of the centre and its range of media to both teachers and students . . .

One implication from the Library Association's statement is the need for a specialist media librarian. The handling of non-print media in some libraries is rather piecemeal. Several sections often share the responsibility and, with the continual pressure to push conventional materials through the system, other media can be neglected. The situation is not eased by the fact that equipment is needed to view and listen to materials, and library staff seem frequently to have an in-built resistance to machines. Photocopying and xerox machines have gained reluctant acceptance, but the advent of new equipment usually causes fresh consternation. There is a good case, too, for a specialist librarian to coordinate the various activities of selection, acquisition, recording, storage and exploitation of both the software materials and their machines. Each library will have its own staff structure, but whatever the position and grade of the media librarian appointed, the need for cooperation between all levels of library staff cannot be stressed too strongly. The situation at North London, as with some other polytechnics, is complicated by the existence of several sites, each with its own library and staff. In this situation, the media resources librarian has been appointed to the central coordinating team, comprised of staff with specialist duties. They work together to formulate policy and to improve the library facilities and services to readers. The creation and use of tape/slide presentations, for example, can involve the media resources librarian, the education and training officer and the information and publications officer, as well as staff on a particular site. Links are made with the sites via the site librarian, and contact is established with academic staff through the team of subject specialists.

Equipment
Non-print materials, with the exception of media such as wall charts, specimens and the like, are useless without their play-back machines. The selection of suitable equipment requires careful thought. Librarians are not expected to be technical experts, so professional advice should be sought. Institutions with educational technology units have the experts to hand. Not only can good advice be obtained, but a standardisation policy can be formulated. This ensures that programmes made by the production unit can be duplicated and deposited in the library without any problem of incompatability. Similarly, media acquired by the library can be played back on any equipment throughout the institution, whether it be in the lecture theatre or seminar room. There is an enormous range of equipment on the market. Manufacturers often design their machines so that only their brand of software can be used. The videotape scene is typical. A tape which has been recorded on an Ampex machine cannot be played on a Sony machine, and vice versa. Similarly, one inch tape cannot be played on a half inch recorder. Consequently, the librarian needs technical advice to avoid these inconsistencies. Where possible, the machines chosen should be of a simple design and as easy to handle and maintain as possible. Thus, on average, cassette play-backs are preferable to reel machines, unless a high standard of sophisticated listening is required.

If one does need outside help, one can consult publications like *Equipment for audio-visual aids*, compiled by the National Audio-Visual Aids Centre, or regularly scan periodicals like *Audio visual, University equipment* and *Visual education*. If convenient, it is worth visiting the National Audio-Visual Aids Centre in London where equipment is on display and professional advice is available. One can also visit a Local

Authority resources centre, such as the ILEA's at Highbury, or any library with a well-established non-print collection. The annual media exhibition at Olympia, Internavex, has a tremendous range of equipment and materials on display. Exhibitions of microform equipment are also staged from time to time. The National Reprographic Centre for documentation provides an excellent service, and their Evaluation Reports are very useful. The price range and quality of equipment is enormous. Sound cassette playback machines only cost a few pounds, while video machines cost several hundred. The final decision taken will naturally depend on the type of media being collected and budgetry constraint.

Acquisition of materials

The materials selected for stock should, of course, reflect the nature of the courses being taught, though some cultural or recreational media may be thought desirable. Again, the budget will, for the most part, dictate the type and range of media bought. Films cost anything from £60 upwards, unrecorded videotapes range from £6 to £18, while sound tapes are only 35p upwards and slides about 15p each.

How does one know what is available? Unfortunately, there is, as yet, no equivalent to the British National Bibliography. Thus, the librarian is forced to collect myriads of catalogues. The number of firms handling non-print materials is enormous, ranging from big publishing organisations to very small agencies. The number increases every year as the newer media gains in popularity. Catalogues of bodies like the Educational Foundation for Visual Aids are worth consulting early on as they include a valuable list of addresses of producers and distributors. One can write off for more catalogues, and the process gradually snowballs. Regular scanning of journals, like *Visual education* and *Audio visual* can bring fresh publishers to light.

Some media are indexed better than others. Film is well covered by such agencies as the British National Film Catalogue, the British Industrial and Scientific Film Association, the British Universities Film Council and the Central Office of Information Film Catalogue. Programmed learning materials are listed in the *APLET yearbook* and in the *Register of programmed instruction*, published by the British Association for Commercial and Industrial Education. Microforms are covered by the annual *Subject guide to microforms in print*, published by Microcard Editions Books, while Xerox University Microfilms issue a catalogue of *Serials in microform*. Gramophone records are listed in the series published by The Gramophone. Other media are not so well documented, and one usually has to look through a host of smaller catalogues to find suitable material. Various agencies are working on the improvement of this situation. The British Universities Film Council, for instance, have extended the scope of their film catalogue to include other non-print materials. This new catalogue, entitled 'Audio-visual materials for higher education', claims to bring together under one cover, non fiction films and other audio-visual materials which are either known to be in use or have been recommended for use in degree courses or research. Arranged in UDC order, each entry gives bibliographical data including technical specifications and a summary of each programme's contents. Distributors' addresses are listed at the back so that a library can easily make contact if a programme seems worth buying or borrowing. Appendix I usefully lists other catalogues, which may be of interest to the media librarian. This catalogue, along with that of the Higher Education Learning Programmes Information Service (HELPIS), which is published by the Council for Educational Technology, provides the main coverage of non-print media at the current time.

Another major selection problem is caused by the predominance of school material that is commercially available. Manufacturers have realised the enormous potential of the school market and so far have concentrated their efforts in that sector. It is a much more complex matter to cater for the needs of institutions of higher education. Courses are very specific and often idiosyncratic and while relevant learning materials can be designed by a member of the teaching staff, it is much more difficult for an outside agency to produce the right material, especially as he has to consider the selling powers of his commodities on the market in general. The apathy generally shown by higher education has done little to encourage the manufacturer, though ironically, this lack of interest from academics has partly resulted from a poor range of commercial materials suited to their needs.

Many catalogues are bibliographically very inadequate, with the exception of the BUFC and HELPIS catalogues already mentioned. Usually, there is only a minimal amount of information given, few technical specifications and no indication of audience level. Thus, unless one writes off for further information or one previews materials, a mistake can be made, and a programme which seemed by its title to be worth acquiring, can turn out to be at a lower educational level. Institutions with teaching studies departments can absorb such materials into the teaching practice library collection. Incidentally, the problem of selecting media for student use on school practice is quite the reverse. There is so much material on the market that one has to rely on reviews in *Visual education* and the *Times educational supplement* for assistance. Selection of materials is most effective when done in cooperation with the teaching staff. Thereby, one hopes that programmes will be recommended to students in the same way as books and journal articles. This is current practice at Brunel University, for example, where students regularly use the library's videotape collection on the advice of their tutors. Unfortunately, this situation is the exception at the moment, but it will become the norm in future.

Where the academic staff is completely disinterested in educational technology, one must act independently and purchase material that appears relevant to the courses being taught. Students, themselves, may help to initiate change. As they emerge from secondary schools where learning resources centres are more fully developed, they will expect to find a provision of similar facilities in the higher education environment. Their suggestions for stock additions are worth encouraging too.

It may be found that members of staff have started collections of their own, and consequently, there is a scattering of resources throughout the whole institution. This has usually occurred because teachers want easy access to materials for teaching. Thus, an art or architecture department may well have a collection of illustrations and slides, a biology or geology department may have specimens and slides, a geography department maps and slides. A worthwhile, but difficult, enterprise, is for the media librarian to discover and list these departmental holdings so that some kind of union catalogue can be compiled for the general benefit of the institution. The circulation of questionnaires to members of staff can help bring this information to light, but on the whole, personal contact is more effective. A tactful approach can inspire staff to donate materials to the library collection, where they are retrievable by both students and staff, but if teachers prefer the materials to be kept departmentally, duplicates can be made and stored in the library for student access.

The major source of programmes will be from the educational technology staff. They are responsible for sponsoring and making programmes and materials for the rest of the academic staff, though they may independently record material which seems worthwhile, copyright being cleared, of course. Duplicates of sound and videotapes can then be prepared for the library collection.

Interlibrary loans
When a programme is only wanted for one occasion, it may not be worth purchasing. Is it possible for libraries to borrow non-print media in the same way as they do books? There is, unfortunately, no clearing house akin to the British Library Lending Division. The major bibliographical tool is the HELPIS catalogue mentioned previously. It lists teaching and learning materials produced in universities, polytechnics and other institutions of higher education in the United Kingdom. The entries are well annotated with summaries of each programme, technical specifications and usually a note on the availability of the material. The Council for Educational Technology has sponsored a similar catalogue of non-print media made by colleges and departments of education, entitled CELPIS, and there is now a HELPIS Medical catalogue. Both are valuable keys to sources of material in the sphere of higher education, but in practice, one finds that the specificity of programmes and the incompatibility of equipment makes borrowing impractical.

An interchange of programmes on a local level where common aims can be worked out and a policy on standardisation agreed upon, may be more profitable. At Newcastle, for example, a cooperative scheme has been initiated. The Newcastle Media Resources Organising Committee (NEMROC) has participants from the univeristy, the polytechnic, the college of education and the city library. They collaborate on policies such as the standardisation of equipment and the interchange of programmes.

The most popular type of media exchange established so far is the hiring of films. This has become standard practice because the purchasing price of films is so high. As they may be only shown once, the payment of a hire charge is more economic. Some libraries do offer a film hiring service to their clientele, but it seems to me to be a more logical function of the educational technology department where the projectionist can check the film, organise its showing and ensure its return undamaged to the parent body. The involvement of the librarian as middle man seems wasteful and unnecessary.

Cataloguing and classification
The items acquired for the library's collection have then to be listed for the maximum convenience of the library users. There is, as yet, no national cataloguing service to assist. There are major catalogues in existence but they vary considerably in the comprehensiveness of their coverage, in their standards of cataloguing and in the frequency of their publication. The

Council for Educational Technology and the British National Bibliography are hoping to effect the cooperation of several organisations such as the British National Film Catalogue, the British Universities Film Council and other major bodies, so that a common pool of information can be created. The proposed name for this amalgamation of data is the British Media Record. The quality of future catalogues, whether they specialise in one format of media or in one particular subject area, should improve. They will be able to draw information from this central pool and consequently, their coverage will be more comprehensive and their catalogue entries standardised.

Meantime, most libraries do their cataloguing at a local level. Non-print media have been quite a headache for librarians in the past, as part III of the Anglo-American Cataloguing Rules was not really adequate. Much deliberation on the problem has produced a new code of practice the non-book cataloguing rules, jointly published by the Library Association and the National Council for Educational Technology in 1973. The implementation of these rules can effect the standardisation of cataloguing not only for the proposed British Media Record but in libraries and resource centres throughout the country. The rules are so constructed that an item can be identified and its physical and technical characteristics described. The standard item description contains the following elements: title statement; statement of primary intellectual responsibility; edition statement; credits; imprint; physical form designator and technical specification; series statement; notes; item number; tracing.

A large proportion of non-print media has no obvious 'author', but where a person or body has primary intellectual responsibility for the creation of an item, that name is added as a heading to the standard item description. The rules also standardise on the terminology used to describe the varying types of media. Thus, the library user can expect a consistency in use of terms like videotape, sound tape, sound disc in the various catalogues and libraries he may use. The technical details given in the catalogue entry enable the user to identify the type of equipment needed to reproduce the media. It is important that he knows, for example, whether the library's collection of sound tapes is on cassette or reel. Details like length of programme or colour specification can also affect his choice. If this information is not available on the container, the cataloguer will have to play the programme through, which is a time consuming process. Unfortunately, one cannot browse through many non-print materials as easily as one can a book. Full details must be given on the catalogue card, therefore, so that the user may be given maximum assistance.

There has been a great deal of discussion on whether entries for print and non-print media should be interfiled in a single catalogue or whether separate catalogues should be compiled. Some librarians consider that users are only interested in one specific type of medium and, consequently, information on other formats of media is irrelevant. If this were absolutely the case, separate catalogues would be worthwhile. But it is hard to discount the advantage to be gained by having information on the library's total resources in one place, particularly as the materials themselves may be scattered throughout the system. Thus a user, seeking for example, a slide-set among entries in a multi media catalogue may find a filmstrip, a set of wallcharts or a book of illustrations an acceptable alternative or, indeed, more suited to his needs. There is a natural reluctance anyway on the part of readers to use the catalogue. A single multi media catalogue may not be too much of a deterrent while an arrary of catalogues may be ignored.

There is divided opinion too on whether coloured cards should be used to differentiate the types of media: blue for slides, pink for sound tapes, for instance. Conventional print media is not so divided. Entries for books, pamphlets, reports or theses are usually all on white cards. The cataloguing information on the card should be sufficiently full and accurate to obviate the need for further guiding. The case against colour coding is quite strong. The variety of media in the library's stock could eventually outnumber the range of colours available. Shades of card sometimes vary slightly, and this may be enough to confuse the reader. The whole exercise is lost on the small but significant percentage of users who are colour-blind. Our aim should be to present information as simply and accurately as possible and the practice of colour coding does not contribute towards this aim.

The classification of non-print media is no more difficult than it is with print media. The difference between a book of photographs of the Eiffel Tower, for example, a filmstrip of the same building, a slide-set or a moving film is in their physical format, not in their information content. In general academic libraries, it is desirable to use the same classification scheme for all materials as this makes retrieval for readers far easier. It is worthwhile repeating the physical form designator of the medium above or below the class mark on the catalogue card to remind the reader of the format of medium being described and its likely location.

Recently amalgamated polytechnics have an additional problem; that of establishing a uniform classification scheme throughout their libraries. This can take some time to achieve. Meantime, it is easier for borrowers if non-print media is classified according to the local scheme. Where there is a large specialised collection, of slides for example, a separate filing order, such as accession number, may make retrieval easier.

Processing and storage

Book processing is a straightforward business, but the physical range of non-print materials creates extra problems. The means of attaching a date label to a filmstrip is not immediately obvious, though one can find ways of circumventing such difficulties. If filmstrips are accompanied by a set of notes, the date label can be affixed to these; if slides are stored in plastic packs, the label can be kept in the plastic pocket or attached by adhesive tape to the back of the pack. When an item can be separated from its container, information such as the classification number, the accession number and the library's identification mark needs to be applied on both. Another problem with the 5 x 5 cm slide is its restricted writing area. A special pencil is required for writing on film. In addition, some materials require extra processing to make them easier to handle by the user. The application of a coloured dot on the side of slides indicating how they should be placed in the projector is a typical example, or the labelling of filmloop containers to differentiate between Standard and Super 8 mm.

Where should the non-print media be kept? The best place is probably in a separate area within the library. When the media are stored in a special room outside the library, there is a danger that the collection will be under exploited because its existence is not immediately obvious. If this situation in unavoidable, through shortage of space for instance, it may be necessary to advertise the service through 'happenings' like exhibitions, film shows or gramophone recitals.

The ideal situation would be to have print and non-print media interfiled in one classified sequence, but this is impracticable. Imagine the difference in physical dimensions between a microfiche, a wallchart, a book and a filmstrip. The non-print items could only be stored with the print if the former were kept in a dummy book container. This is already done with some sound tapes, such as those published by Sussex Tapes and the Open University, and if these were the only type of non-print media in the collection, it would be perfectly valid to interfile them with the books.

The solution adopted by most multi-media libraries is to opt for separate storage, according to format. Special shelves and cabinets have been designed to accommodate the ever varying types of media. Clear labels and notices need to be affixed to give users maximum guidance as to what is stored where.

A fundamental decision linked to the storage of media is whether the materials and equipment should be on closed or open access. Closed access is a safeguard against damage or theft, but the open display of materials is far more attractive to the library user. Non-print media are under used as yet, so if the librarian can make his materials as accessible as possible, he may help to promote their use. Curiosity is a fundamental part of human nature, and an open invitation to browse may lead to eventual use. Large scale theft can be avoided by ensuring there is a librarian on duty in the media area, and it is always possible to lock cabinets and secure equipment to tables.

The physical conditions in the media area also require careful consideration. High temperatures can affect videotapes and films, for instance, while excessive light, dust and humidity are bad for slides. Non-print media tend to be more delicate materials and are less resilient to physical conditions than books. Their handling, too, requires careful attention. Instructions on their use can be placed alongside the playback equipment.

Some libraries opt for having carrels specially fitted with equipment. The Surrey Carrel and Devans Tutor, designed for viewing tape/slide presentations are useful. If the range of play-back machines is fairly extensive, however, it is simpler to have equipment like video-tape recorders and monitors, sound cassette machines, or microfiche readers on tables, so that the user can replay the media in similar conditions to the way he would read books or journal articles. An open plan with equipment in full view may help to remove some of the awe and anxiety which, unfortunately, seems attached to media resources. A library user may well be attracted to viewing a video-tape cassette if he sees his colleague plugging in his own programme and watching. Sound problems can be overcome by the use of headphones.

Information and exploitation
It is not sufficient merely to collect media resources. A publicity campaign usually has to be launched to encourage their use, and there are several ways of doing this. One can regularly distribute information on new programmes and materials to members of staff. Manufacturers' catalogues are usually free, so it is an easy matter to obtain duplicates.

Leaflets and brochures such as those issued by radio and television companies can be sent round to departments, and posters advertising programmes and exhibitions can be displayed on notice-boards.

Another means of publicising the library and its collection is to mount media exhibitions. The location of such displays is important. If, for example, a circulation area, like the entrance hall is chosen, the impact is greater and the whole venture more effective, as staff and students are more or less forced to take notice. Typical reaction is one of surprise that the library has acquired such resources and has such services to offer. Some academics may not have made wide use of the library for some time and have little idea of recent developments. A lot of students seem unaware that these resources are intended for their use. The play-back equipment can be put on display so that visitors have a chance to operate it in what they may feel to be a more relaxed atmosphere than that prevailing in the library. Distribution of a bulletin or hand-out can summarise the total library service and act as a reminder when they have left the exhibition.

As well as staging multi-media events, one can also promote the use of a single type of medium. A school of librarianship, for example, could arrange a show of tape/slide presentations relevant to students about to sit an examination. More relaxed occasions could include a series of gramophone record recitals.

A more formal channel of communication is through committees. Each institution will have its own particular network and library representation on these can create new and sometimes influential contacts. Representatives on these committees will come from various faculties, the media resources unit and the library, to discuss and formulate policies relating to the use of media resources throughout the whole institution. The library has a chance to report on its progress and can contribute to the discussions and decisions being made.

Direct communication with departments can be achieved in cooperation with the subject specialist team. It is most helpful if the media librarian can be invited to staff meetings so that library policy relating to media can be fully explained and some useful feedback obtained. The new polytechnics tend to have large academic staffs, and it can take a long time to establish wide personal contacts. Informal gatherings may supply the chance of giving the library some publicity in a more relaxed and possibly more receptive atmosphere.

Training

There is usually only one media librarian per institution, and it is therefore imperative, particularly in the multi-site situation, that other library staff are conversant with non-print materials and their play-back equipment. Practical training sessions where staff can handle hardware and software are essential because they, in turn, will need to instruct the academic staff and students in the absence of the media librarian. There should be no mystique or apprehension surrounding the use of equipment. Televisions, cassette players and other devices are familiar in the home. Their presence in the library should not cause consternation.

Finally, it is worth pointing out the positive role the library can play in the actual production of media resources. Though the responsibility for the technical creation of media remains with the educational technology staff, the library can, as do other departments, actively sponsor the production of media. Perhaps the most familiar type of media produced so far is tape/slide presentations. Many libraries, including Trent Polytechnic, Newcastle as well as North London, have produced guides to their services. These are normally shown to new students as part of their introductory session on the library, though they can view the programme again individually in the library if they so desire.

Subject guides could also be created, such as the introduction to the literature of law, librarianship and geology compiled by the staff at the Polytechnic of North London. Similar programmes are listed in the HELPIS catalogue. The subject guides are normally shown to students later in their courses. Though we have shown our programmes as part of a group teaching session, they are available in the library for re-play whenever a student so wishes. Tape/slide guides on the literature of various subjects are currently being sponsored by SCONUL. Some ten programmes were produced in the first round, and a second round of productions is now under way. OSTI is supporting an evaluation project on their effectiveness. Polytechnic and university libraries are participating in the scheme and the programmes being designed cover such ground as: how to use *Science citation index,* an introduction to the literature of biology, and the use of periodicals and their indexes. Each of these presentations will eventually be shown to a student audience and a survey on the effectiveness of each programme will be conducted. The result of these tests will be analysed and the programmes will be re-written where necessary. As a general principle, student learning packages should undergo regular assessment and the programmes revised if they are no longer achieving their objectives.

Other libraries have used different types of media to publicise their services and instruct their readers. The School of Navigation, part of the City of London Polytechnic, has an introduction to its library on videotape. Hatfield Polytechnic has a film on the library service. They also have an induction loop system, consisting of pre-recorded tapes on specific bibliographic tools. The user simply has to put on special earphones and he can move freely around examining the books in question as he is listening to the tape.

Thus there is great potential for librarians in this field to involve themselves not only in collecting a range of media resources, as part of their service to staff and students, but they can exploit these resources to promote and publicise other aspects of the library service and instruct our readers to gain maximum benefit from them.

Stock revision

So far, I have concentrated on procedures for adding materials to stock and establishing media as part of the library service. Revision of stock must not be overlooked as it is important if the library is to maintain high standards. All items added to the library's collection will have been carefully examined, and the process of cataloguing and classifying should have weeded out any unsuitable materials, whether they be of inappropriate educational level or poor technical quality. This principle applies to home-produced media as well as commercial acquisitions. It may seem tactless to refuse a set of slides offered to the library by a well-meaning member of staff, but if their technical standard is poor, they should be rejected.

As with books, one must make it a positive policy to weed out material that is obsolescent, or when the wear and tear of regular use makes it an impediment to the user. We discard books beyond repair; damaged wallcharts and scratched gramophone records must be given the same treatment. The stock needs frequent attention. Ironically, even when media, such as videotapes, are not being used, they need to be played through at intervals to help preserve their quality.

Conclusion

Institutions of higher education have, on the whole, been slow to appreciate the potential of the non-book media. Though librarians have reflected this conservative attitude, they are, in fact, in a strong position to initiate change. The new polytechnics, in particular, can play an effective role in this. They have no set pattern of tradition to follow. With the design of new courses, there is a unique opportunity for experimenting with new methods of teaching and learning. Where courses are interdisciplinary, specially designed programmes can help achieve basic levels of learning. The library can house such packages as part of its stock of resources. The CNAA itself have realised the importance of the library's contribution, and they have been known to reject proposed new courses if the library's stock was not felt to be adequate. Such official pressure as this can result in an increase in the library's grant and subsequent improvement of resources.

This has presented a special opportunity for the introduction of non-print materials. Students on degree courses need access to back runs of journals which polytechnic libraries have not previously maintained. The use of microfilm in this context enables the library to save on money and storage space, both of which are at a premium. The emphasis in polytechnics has often been on practical subjects. Consequently, a medium such as television can, on occasions, be a more effective teaching vehicle than the lecture and text book. Language departments recognise the value of recorded material and the library can support this by building up a collection of foreign tapes and records. The staff and students of education can draw upon the enormous range of non-print media currently being produced for school consumption.

The acquisition of such materials presents libraries with the opportunity of playing an active role in the promotion of effective learning. We are ideally placed to look after the new media, to catalogue and index them, issue and recall them and to promote their use by both staff and students.

CHAPTER V

Teaching library use

Nancy Hammond

LIBRARIANS IN THE United Kingdom and the United States have been talking and writing about the need for reader instruction for many years. Considering the number of articles that have been written, it would appear that such instruction is a long established tradition on both sides of the Atlantic. Once we begin to read through the literature however, we find that almost all programmes which are discussed are mainly ideas yet to be tested and accepted, or programmes that have been put to use for the first time. Perhaps we might decide that those who have ongoing programmes are not writing about them. But then, if we delve a bit deeper and ask any group of people who have completed their higher education if they ever, during their student years, were given anything more than a tour of the library, the usual answer is in the negative. There are librarians both in this country and in the US who have made or are making reader instruction programmes work. Therefore, you would expect to find some people who have had experience of library instruction and yet, it must be a very small percentage of all those students who graduate. Even where the tradition of reader instruction is well established, the pattern throughout any one polytechnic is usually varied and ranges from some departments having no instruction through to a very few who are appreciative of a series of well planned programmes covering all stages of the student's progress within his chosen field. The significant factor about these few well established programmes is that the type, scope, and success of the entire scheme often depends entirely on the personality of the librarian who does the teaching. Almost without exception the successful reader instruction programme ends when the librarian who established it moves on to a new post.

One of the major reasons for this state of affairs is that library schools do very little to train future librarians for the job of teaching library use. In addition, the experience of a librarian in his own schooling has probably never included having a librarian who was someone with an important skill to be taught to all students. It is no wonder then that few librarians come to a post with any background or experience of reader instruction.

Two distinct types of organisation for reader instruction are emerging in the polytechnics today. The first is the tutor librarian whose major task is teaching. He is usually responsible for all teaching within a polytechnic or divides this responsibility with other tutor librarians. He is generally expected to devise his own teaching programmes and promote them among the departments to which he has been assigned.

There are advantages and disadvantages in this system. The tutor librarian can spend a good part of his time in preparation and should therefore be able to present an interesting and well planned programme. He also is on more of an equal footing with other teaching staff and may, therefore, with a bit of tact, manage to become an accepted teacher with whom the lecturers are willing to work. However on the minus side are all the problems of being a teacher among librarians. Many of the library staff will tend to resent the tutor librarian's more flexible schedule. Perhaps the greatest problem however is that in serving several departments the tutor librarians are not frequently to be found at a central information point in the library and consequently much of the benefit of getting to know the students in the classroom is lost. The tutor librarians are not readily available to help users on a one to one basis and this important part of the teaching process is left to the information officers or library assistants.

The second way in which reader instruction is being organised is to make it part of the job of the subject specialist librarian. In this case there is considerable advantage in having the programmes coordinated by a senior librarian in charge of library teaching for the entire polytechnic. The advantage of this system is that the work of creating a close liaison with departments becomes a total one for the subject specialist. The central coordinator can be called in to help develop programmes and prepare any teaching aids. He can work with the subject specialist in the actual teaching and help present a team effort when there is some advantage in this approach. In addition the coordinator is in a position to give the academic staff an overall picture of the sort of programmes which have been developed for other departments as well as what might be done to meet their particular needs.

The disadvantage of the subject specialist is that teaching is only one part of a very demanding job. Providing reader instruction is not only time consuming in itself but alo creates even more work by making students and staff into better library users. With centralised coordination of the teaching programmes it should be possible to attack the various problems in two ways.

The academic staff member gets to know his subject specialist and comes to regard him as someone with a particularly helpful type of subject knowledge. In many cases with the additional enthusiasm of the coordinator helping with an instruction programme, academic staff may be won over to the ideas put forward by the specialist and coordinator together. The problem of personality conflicts should not be overlooked and where one person may not be able to communicate well with certain staff members, another person may get along quite well.

The problem of the newly appointed subject specialist who has never taught and feels unsure of his ability in this area can be greatly helped by having someone to turn to for assistance in preparing the materials to be presented, and, in some cases, to do the greater part of the actual teaching. The subject specialist should always take some part in the teaching from the very beginning. In my experience after several sessions of seeing how the coordinator presents the material, and having made some small initial contribution, such as explaining a specific information source he knows particularly well, the subject specialist will have gained the necessary confidence to take over the bulk of the teaching.

Two views on the actual presentation frequently combine to make a better programme overall. The combination of subject background on the part of the specialist and the coordinator's experience with various types of library instruction should make for excellent results. Both these systems using tutor librarians or subject specialists, have their good points, but in my estimation in the long run the subject specialist method should work better. One reason for this is that with centralised coordination it can be more a part of a general on going programme that does not stand or fall because of the personality of one person. It also has the advantage of giving a department one person who they can get to know and rely on in all aspects of their use of the library. In this way the library service as a whole can be seen with its various parts relating to one another.

Setting up a programme
How do we, then, set up a programme that will become an integral part of the syllabus in each department?

One of the worst things that can happen is that after the department has given the time, the reader instruction is done poorly. Librarians have a tendency to expect the student to take in a mass of detail in a short time. Frequently, we insist that the first thing that must be learned is the classification scheme. Student reaction has shown, however, that the intricacies of Dewey are of little interest. Most students of librarianship find this area of limited appeal and it is unreasonable to present other than the merest outline to students of other subjects. The important thing for students to learn, it would seem, is how to use the subject index to the card catalogue. Once this is mastered it will not matter whether they understand the class numbers or not. In most cases, the more inquisitive student will ask what the numbers mean and a short explanation at that time is probably the best way to get this information across.

Another reason to avoid 'teaching' classification schemes is that they are extremely difficult to defend when someone decides to attack them. As librarians we may agree that classifying all of knowledge is a difficult task and we will have to make do with the efforts that have been made. Trying to explain this to students who want to know why all the books they need for their course are not under one number, is almost impossible. There is evidence that not all librarians would agree with this assessment but I think the quickest way to bore students and leave oneself open to attacks from academic staff is by insisting on discussion of classification in some detail. My advice is to keep your knowledge of classification schemes to yourself until someone asks for an explanation.

Unfortunately most teaching librarians must spend their time trying to get their programmes accepted. Without several years experience behind you it is difficult to envisage ever getting more than one chance to see each group during the entire undergraduate course. If time on library instruction is to be severely limited then we must ensure that we make the most of the initial opportunity and hope that its success will generate further interest. The first thing we should try to establish is that basic library information is provided in a guidebook available to all students when they enter the library. Usually students must register with the library in order to take out books. Therefore, during the first week of term they will most likely enter the library, have a chance to look around, and be issued with a copy of the guide. Because of the number of new people and new places introduced to the student during his first week at college, it would be better to put off the introductory library talk until a few weeks into term. By that time the students may realise that they do need some help. This introduction should be viewed mainly as a way for the student to get to know the librarians who will be able to help him. It is more important that the student finds out that the librarian is there to help and is quite willing to do so, than to learn how to use the card catalogue or the intricacies of the classification scheme.

In whatever way this talk is presented, either as informal instruction using the library guide as a handout, or with a tape slide guide or other audio visual presentation, it should be short and to the point. It should be presented in a friendly and, if possible, humorous way. Its main purpose should basically be the message that the staff is quite human and approachable and are there to help users. The student should be encouraged to present his library problems to the subject specialist.

If we do manage to get this message across, students will not be slow to ask for help. Once contact with students has been established it will provide real evidence of what the student needs. If you can go to the teaching staff and suggest that because a number of students have come to you with the same type of information problems then perhaps it would be appropriate to plan further library instruction or to ask a lecturer to present some basic information within the context of his own teaching. This need not take a whole class period and if the staff member sees the relevance of this it could become a viable part of his teaching programme in the future.

This brings us to a difficult and very important aspect of reader instruction, timing. Learning to use library resources effectively is a skill which students will readily appreciate if it is presented to them at a time when they can see its merit, for instance when they can use this skill immediately on a project in hand. The only possible way to find out the exact moment when the students will be receptive is to have a good working relationship with the students and with their lecturers. Hopefully, as programmes are accepted by academic staff, they will be able to advise as to when the instruction should come.

The teaching librarian in discussing timing with academic staff can give some further indication from his own experience as to when students will find a library course, beyond that of basic guidance, most useful. It is important to reach the student when he has had time to make some use of the library, preferably at a time when a major project is to be prepared. If the assignment of the project coincides with an explanation of the techniques of literature searching within the library, the students are usually highly receptive. It is perhaps worthwhile to preface the presentation with a few remarks about saving the students a lot of time. Frequently students who have done a paper without any previous instruction have encountered substantial difficulties. Once they are aware of pitfalls, students can be extremely receptive if the material is presented in a manner clearly related to the difficulties of project planning. It is most gratifying to have a student realise the value of such instruction. Early in their courses many students experience frustration in trying to assemble useful information for the extended essay of a project. Consequently, a library course judiciously designed to help them at just the right moment is likely to capture the interest of the students.

Relations with academic staff

One of the biggest difficulties to be overcome is that of the attitude of the teaching staff. Most academic staff when approached concerning instruction for their students, if they are willing at all, will immediately begin discussing how and when the library course can be slotted in the term's work.

This idea of 'the library lecture', aptly described by Millicent C Palmer as the 'ghost of library instruction past', is frequently nervously received, particularly by academic staff who have not been impressed by previous efforts. It is essential to explain exactly what is to be done. It must be kept in mind that it is unlikely that the staff member was ever given any sort of reader instruction during the years before becoming a lecturer. There seem to be two distinct attitudes from academic staff who do not accept the idea of library instruction. One is that if he could learn how to use the library himself there was no reason why a student today should not be expected to do the same thing. The second is that some lecturers do not want students digging out all sorts of things seen as having little relevance to the course.

The first of these attitudes can be challenged on the ground that the information explosion being what it is, the student nowadays is faced with a confusing array of material which requires a minimum of explanation if it is to be used effectively. Also most students are probably not as confident as staff expect. Therefore it is unlikely that they have ever summoned up the courage to ask a librarian what is available, or even more likely, that they have never even realised the extent of the literature available.

The second attitude is difficult to cope with in any direct way. Academic staff who feel nervous that students might probe into areas deemed to be inappropriate are obviously rather uncertain of the value of instruction which encourages the student to do so. But while the librarian is obviously concerned with helping the student to improve his ability to use information tools, it is also the case that examples used can be designed to fit usefully into the pattern of studies or can be related to problems the student is facing at work or in college. The member of staff is more likely to be assured of the value of library instruction if the subject specialist can take especial interest in any research the staff member is conducting. The librarian may find the time to scan indexes and abstracts with an eye to these special interests. Attention should be drawn to relevant journal articles and new book titles and the lecturer should be made aware of new reference tools covering his subject area. This special service to staff probably will take extra time that will not always be available but it will usually pay off in the end. If these efforts fail with some it will still be possible to establish good relationships and a working programme with others in the department. Then it can be hoped that highly motivated students, who have not had access to library instruction, will hear from their fellow students about the library programme and perhaps either come direct to the library for help or go to their lecturer and ask why they have not received library instruction.

It is often difficult to keep things in perspective and not get terribly depressed if you are not successful at first. The problems and the obstacles in many places are so great that it can take years to establish the type of programme you would like to have.

Presentation

Introductory material about how to use the library in general can be dealt with in many ways depending on the number of students to be seen. Time can be saved in the long run by putting such information on to a tape slide guide or in a film presentation. The initial preparation is time consuming but there is a substantial literature on the subject of tape slide presentation, and librarians who have experimented are usually willing to share their experience. Such assistance is extremely valuable but it is only through trial and error that the librarian can eventually produce a guide suited to local need. Of course, one great advantage of this particular vehicle of communication is the ease with which it can be edited to allow for change.

If this presentation is done well and gives a clear and friendly picture of the library it might have more impact than a short talk from a librarian. Our society is well attuned to films and television and it is more likely that a good presentation of this type would be more effective than a twenty minute lecture. Opinions differ on the ideal length of such a presentation but extensive experience at North London suggests that a twelve to fifteen minute programme is about right. Librarians tend to feel that they cannot get across all the important things a students needs to know in such a short time, but it has been found that students fail to absorb detail when the tape slide goes on too long.

Of course, a traditional and perhaps essential part of the introduction is a library tour. In planning this it must be noted that much of the detail will not be remembered. The most important thing is to create an image of the library as a friendly place where the staff is always willing to help. The basic library tour need not be part of the student induction week, in fact, such is the mass of information presented at these times, there is some benefit in delaying the introduction to the library. Hopefully, students will be more receptive once they have settled into the first term and are beginning to feel a need to use the library. The impact of the tour is strengthened by the provision of attractively designed and concisely written library guides or similar publications.

Ideally any further instruction will take place within the library walls. Polytechnics with new library buildings have taken this into consideration by setting aside space for this purpose. Some boast both small seminar rooms as well as one large, well-equipped library classroom. This arrangement allows for maximum flexibility in dealing with groups of varying sizes. The provision of such teaching facilities is in no sense wasteful of space as it will allow the library to develop its teaching programmes without artificial hindrance and will provide staff with accommodation for their own training programmes, committee and working party meetings. However, if such an area does not exist this is no reason to give up the idea of using some quiet area of the library for teaching purposes. This may sound unreasonable to librarians of the 'quiet library' school but an interesting, well received programme can make it worthwhile. Before instruction begins, notices can be put on the main door and on the tables and desks to alert other students of the times when there will be groups in the library for instruction. In one small library where this was done, students who were studying in the library at the time asked if they could join the group.

By using a part of the library the student can be shown the exact locations of most items to be discussed. This also solves the problem of carrying large numbers of reference tools to a lecture room borrowed from a teaching department. Even when a well equipped library classroom is available, it is still very important to introduce students into the library itself for practical work once the introductory instruction has been given.

If it is necessary to use a lecture room in another part of the building the best solution may be to take along a limited selection of the most interesting and essential tools, and to supplement these with colour slides and other visual aids. More important still is to arrange students into small groups of five to fifteen, if this can be negotiated. With this size of group the various reference books, indexes, etc can easily be passed around the room and everyone can be given a chance to see what they look like and how to use them. Library classrooms can usefully contain superseded numbers of periodical indexes, abstract services and other reference books which are always there to be used for teaching purposes. However these teaching sets should be kept as up to date as possible, as students unfamiliar with particular items will find it difficult to recognise the latest editions on the shelf if teaching sets become too dated and of a different format.

It is important to remember that after the talk session, students should be taken into the library to use the tools on the shelves. Where several items are being discussed a small group can easily be split up and dispersed among several areas to look at indexes, abstracts or bibliographies without seriously disrupting the work of others.

The value of the tape slide introduction to the library has already been mentioned, but this form of presentation has proved to be equally valuable as a means of introducing the literature of a subject to undergraduates. Several excellent presentations of this sort have been prepared at the Polytechnic of North London, notably for the materials of geography and law. Once again, care should be taken to avoid too much detail and the tape slide will have to be supplemented with handouts, discussion and practical exercises in the library itself. But the sequence of slides showing the shelf, the book, and then contents list and specimen page frequently assist in the effective introduction of a new and important reference work. Skilful use of the overhead projector, film and film loop should all be considered as possible aids, particularly in a situation where the library is supported by a good education technology unit which is able to offer appropriate advice and assistance.

Finally, there is a great deal to be said for the subject specialist seeking the help of both library and teaching colleagues to ensure appropriate content and teaching methods when planning library courses. When the needs of a subject are paramount, advice on coverage can be sought from those teaching the students' course, and it might be useful on occasion to combine forces in presenting subject material. Team teaching or joint assessment of teaching can add vitality to a programme. A good description of alternatives to lecturing is given in Donald A Bligh's *What's the use of lectures?* (Penguin 1972).

Training of teaching librarians

As stated before, library schools, for the most part, do little to train future librarians for the task of teaching library use. One or two lectures devoted to reader instruction is the most that any student of librarianship can expect. If the trend towards greater service to readers continues the library schools will eventually have to offer an option of a teaching methods course. In this way at least those librarians who think they would like to teach would have the opportunity to gain some prior experience before taking a post involving teaching duties. Courses could be developed for teaching library use, which must, if we are to have any success, be quite different from those teaching librarianship. If this could be done, the difficulties facing the librarian would be alleviated in the sense that someone facing a group of students for the first time would at least be aware of the rudiments of technique and presentation. The confidence instilled through training might at least enable him to stand up in front of a group and get across some basic information about the library.

As this training is not now provided in library school, we must make use of existing courses dealing with teaching methods in general. Most polytechnics now have some sort of in-service training course for new lecturers. Evidence of this can be found in Alan Harding's *Training of polytechnic teachers* published in 1974 by the Society for Research into Higher Education. There is no reason why librarians who intend to teach should not join these basic courses provided by their own polytechnics. In most cases they will occupy a few days just before beginning of autumn term.

However, some polytechnics do offer longer term programmes. In the case of Hatfield Polytechnic there is a one week induction course for all new lecturers who wish to attend. This is followed by a one year in-service course, meeting one day a week during term time. The most helpful event during the first week is the opportunity to give a fifteen minute lecture to the other in-service trainees. As the first few talks are the most difficult for someone with no public speaking experience, this opportunity to present a talk to a group of people in exactly the same situation as the newly appointed teaching librarian provides the measure of empathy and understanding helpful to a beginner.

The one day a week sessions during the year include valuable guidance on teaching methods, with ample time being given to forms of presentation other than the lecture. Extensive coverage is offered on the use of audio visual aids, the advantages of team teaching and the study of informal methods of presentation. Hopefully, in the future, informal teaching in the library area will predominate, but at this point in time many will think in terms of the straight library lecture as opposed to other methods of guiding students.

Lengthy courses of in-service training might not be possible for a subject specialist librarian, such will be the pressure of other duties. However in the case of the tutor librarian, whose time will be substantially committed to teaching and teaching preparation, attendance on these courses should be given top priority.

Another possibility for the training of teaching librarians is for the polytechnic library to set up its own short courses. These could involve outside speakers, including educational technologists and experienced teachers who would be invited to discuss their ideas on motivation, presentation and appraisal. In addition, library staff with teaching experience would be encouraged to share their ideas with colleagues and to discuss openly problems of likely solutions.

This second type of training worked well in a training session at the Polytechnic of North London for subject specialist librarians. Short talks were given by two staff members with some experience in teaching library use. The first contribution was a general presentation of why the library should extend its reader services to include instruction. This was followed by a surprising discussion when several members of staff expressed their frustration at having spent considerable time preparing an introductory tape slide guide and supporting teaching only to find that some of the academic staff would not concede even half an hour of their class time for their students to participate. It was obvious that some librarians who had been keen to try reader instruction had been seriously discouraged by this resistance from academic staff. Because of other pressures on the subject specialist, it is easy to see why this sort of reception led to a reluctance on the part of the inexperienced librarian to persist with the idea of trying to establish a teaching programme.

The second contributor explained how she had made some headway during a first year as tutor librarian, despite the difficulties placed in her way. This led to those among the staff who had had successes over the years, discussing how they had overcome some of the problems. It appeared that this latter discussion turned the mood of despair engendered by the earlier discussion into one of hopefulness. There seemed to be a renewed willingness to go out and try again and a realisation that a programme of reader instruction accepted by the academic staff need not happen overnight.

It should also be remembered that local efforts in teacher training can be supplemented by outside institutions offering the short courses open to anyone wishing to learn more about teaching methods. One example of this is the University of London Institute of Education which periodically offers courses on lecturing and public speaking. Garnett College has long specialised in the training of teaching staff in further education and offers a special course for tutor librarians.

It is essential if polytechnic libraries hope to set up good reader instruction programmes that the librarian faced with the teaching be given as much help as possible to gain teaching skills. The type of training utilised will depend on the time and money available. However, there is no reason for the librarian teaching for the first time to be deprived of the benefit of some knowledge of first principles. The chances to learn are many and should not be ignored.

We must remember that it is essential when trying to establish a programme of reader instruction throughout the college that it should be presented efficiently on the first occasion. There is nothing more calculated to destroy all hopes of future development of library instruction than the unimpressive first attempt. The hope should be that at least a minority of students will recognise the benefit of the instruction and should not be discouraged by low teaching skills.

Teaching aids

If we agree that our three major problems in setting up reader instruction programmes are: 1) difficulty in convincing academic staff of the importance of reader instruction and also in explaining exactly what is to be taught; 2) the reluctance of many librarians to appear before a group and teach; and 3) the fear of boring the less-motivated student who will fail to see the importance of such instruction.

One solution for making some headway on all three of these problems is to create a humorous but purposeful handout which can be used to: 1) explain basic aims and content; 2) act as a seminar outline for the teaching librarian who is undermined by nervousness; and 3) capture student interest from the beginning.

To illustrate this idea, here are examples from some handouts which have been used successfully in two polytechnics. For most of them the same format was used, that of a literature search. The following basic points were emphasised:

'1) Define your topic—understand what you are researching (use dictionaries, encyclopedias, handbooks, text books, etc.)
   a. Topic must be narrowed down to something manageable.
   b. Definition should include: 1) Decision on period to be covered; 2) Type of materials to be included; 3) Completeness of finished list desired;
   c. Once the subject is clearly defined—begin to compile a bibliography.
2) Determine related subjects.
   a. Books on the more general subject often include material on its parts.
   b. As you proceed, compile as list of terms used in connection with the topic used in indexes. Include synonyms and transatlantic variations in spelling and terminology.
   c. Reproduce references to books and articles accurately; 1) noting name of publisher is a guide to country of origin and standard of scholarship; 2) Including source of reference makes finding original reference possible.
3) Check library subject index for classification numbers.
4) What materials can be traced through the library catalogue in the subject? (books, pamphlets, reports).
   a. Go to the shelves and browse in the subject area.
5) What about periodical articles? Consult abstracts and indexes appropriate to the subject.
   a. Remember time gap between published indexes and time of search.
   b. Browse through most likely recent periodicals.
6) For more books on the subject, check national and subject bibliographies.
7) Check to see if there is any existing research on the subject.
8) Are there any special libraries?
9) What trade associations, professional bodies, research associations are there?
10) Any useful contacts?'

Each of these points is illustrated with excerpts from the appropriate tools. In addition I usually include the annotation about the source from Walford's *Guide to reference material* or one from any other suitable guide. At the end of the booklet is a one page summary of the points covered, an index to the materials which have been illustrated, and a list of credits for drawings and annotations.

In every case choose a topic relevant to the field of study of the students to be seen. In this way basic tools as well as special subject sources can be brought out. The topics I have used were chosen for various reasons. The Harris tweed industry for business studies because I was personally interested in handwoven textiles, Gypsies for social studies because I drove past a gypsy camp on my way home one evening, pubs for environmental design as I felt this might have a universal appeal. In all cases, personal experience and choice happily linked up with student studies or interests. Experience suggests that the time spent has been well rewarded by the enthusiastic reception by the staff and students of material they readily see to be pointed, relevant and succinctly put.

The most time consuming element involved in the process of preparation is the finding and selecting of various line drawings and cartoons which relate to the points to be emphasised and are illustrative of library coverage of the topic in question. In my first attempts, I tried a few free hand drawings with varying results. I could see in the long run this would not work as I was not particularly artistically inclined. As I was at that time scanning periodicals for indexing, I frequently found advertisements illustrated with humorous drawings and kept a file of copies of any I thought to be especially good. I also found that children's books were excellent sources of drawings on almost any subject. At some point, I began to use some of my favourite Peanuts cartoons by Charles M Schulz, and these have been particularly well received by students. Snoopy, Charlie Brown and company have said a lot of wonderfully wise things over the years, and there have been a number of strips dealing specifically with libraries. These could be used in any of the handouts. In addition there are many dealing with books and reading, eg Linus trying to decide on an appropriate volume in which to press his autumn leaves; Lucy being disappointed because Snoopy is not as bright as she first expected because he moves his lips when he reads; and Charlie Brown staying up all night to read *Gulliver's travels* because he has put it off until the last minute and must hand in his book report that day.

Once you get the idea of using cartoons and drawings in this way, you frequently see things which can be incorporated into handouts. One word of caution, note where you found them for the list of acknowledgements at the end of the handout. In most cases, copying a drawing to be

a. Literature Search

mnb
10-74

1. Define your topic
— understand what you are researching
USE:
DICTIONARIES
ENCYCLOPAEDIAS
HAND BOOKS
TEXTBOOKS

from the Encyclopaedia Britannica p. 794-797

Encyclopaedia articles include these references and often bibliographies

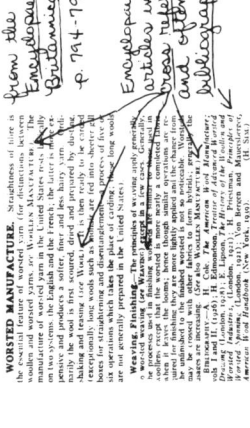

Plate 7: Literature search handout. Original size 295mm x 210mm.

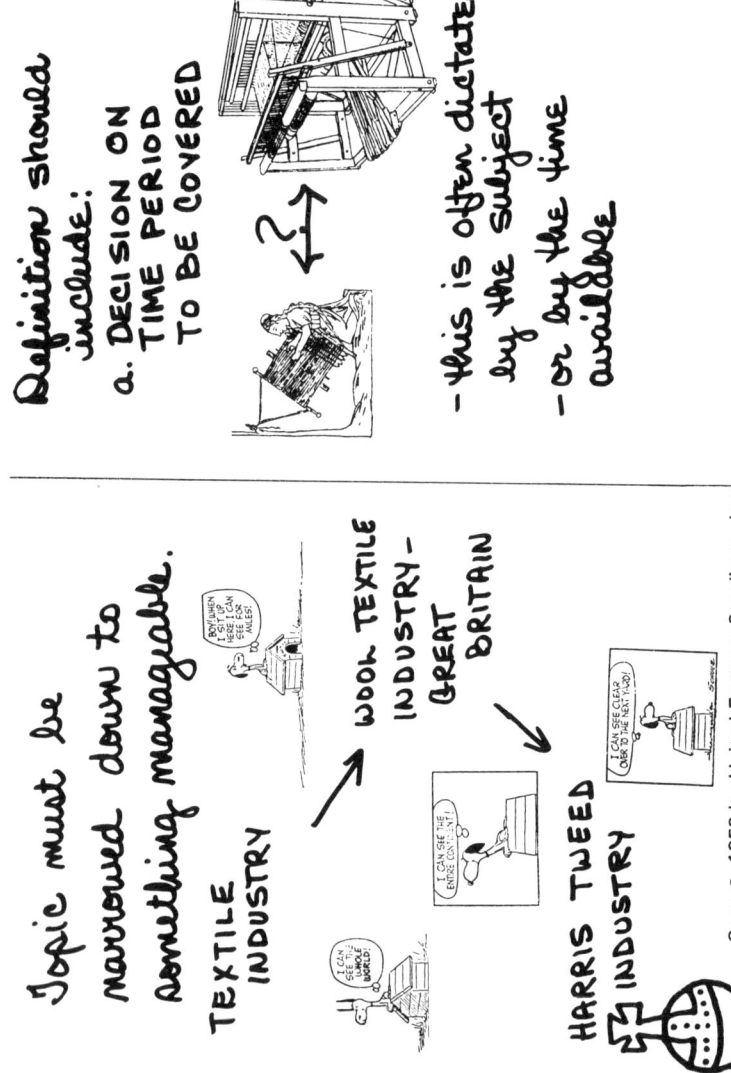

Plate 7: Literature search handout. Original size 295mm x 210mm.

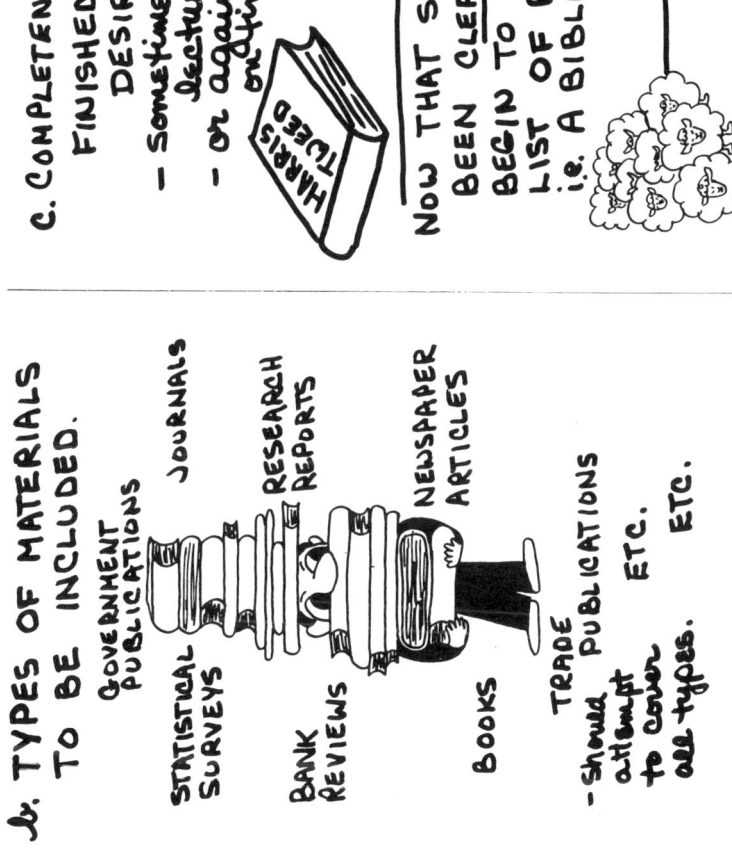

Plate 7: Literature search handout. Original size 295mm x 210mm.

incorporated into an unpublished booklet will not be an infringement of copyright. However, Charles Schulz does like to know where his cartoons are being used. In most cases he will grant permission. In Great Britain permission for use of Peanuts cartoons is given by United Features Syndicate at United Press International, 8 Bouvier Street, London EC4.

The reason I have dealt so thoroughly with this one method of teaching is that there are, at this time. very few polytechnics with well developed reader instruction programmes for their students. Most are only just beginning and as stated earlier, successes in the past have frequently been due to the personality of the librarian who did the teaching. Perhaps this fairly thorough explanation of one method of instruction will be of some help to other teaching librarians trying to start reader instruction programmes in their institutions.

Having discussed the problems of how, when and where we can teach students and staff to use the library, some people may still question the validity and usefulness of this work. Some librarians may challenge the value of such activity because of their low opinion of themselves as librarians, or because they just have too much to do in the day to day running of the library. Teaching is seen by some to be a fringe activity low down on the list of priorities.

To assume that students do not benefit from such instruction because the initial response is poor is to accept defeat too soon. As has been said, there are very few people anywhere who have ever experienced a good reader instruction programme. It is a new experience for students, staff and librarians as well.

Without sounding too idealistic about it, I can say that I believe that learning to use a library can be one of the most important skills acquired during student years. If during the period of formal education students experienced a really good introduction to the resources of a library, they would realise that questions in everyday life can often be answered quickly by a visit to the local library.

More to the point, as trained librarians we must all have experienced seeing a particular source for the first time and wishing it had been known earlier. The student who makes any attempt to write a good essay or submit a worthwhile project must waste considerable time if he is not aware of the basic sources available to him. To say that all the student has to do is ask the librarian for help assumes that he must believe that the person sitting behind a pile of books or busily checking things in the card catalogue is thoroughly approachable. The evidence available on this score is that most students do not see the librarian as a particularly communicative person, but as one who deals in mysterious arts completely unexplainable to the ordinary mortal. In fact, one major opportunity to destroy this image comes with the setting up of programmes of library instruction. Students are much more willing to ask for help from their subject specialist in the library once they have seen him in action as a teacher.

This brings me to the problem of the librarian who sees himself as the 'guardian of knowledge' and the only person who can be trusted to find the relevant information. If all students were confident extroverts, our guardians of knowledge would be inundated for twenty four hours a day trying to supply the right information for every student. If we are to offer higher quality education to increasing numbers of students, who will inevitably come into contact with large library resources, then there is a good case for encouraging self help by providing adequate instruction designed both to bring the librarian and student into contact with each other and to motivate the student towards purposeful use of library services and materials. The ultimate value of this teaching will be further evidenced by the student's confident use of library resources in a working situation and for the purposes of research or personal development. Library instruction, in these terms, can truly be seen as a useful, long term investment.

PART 2

Subject specialisation

CHAPTER VI

Introduction and survey

Martin Walker

ANY CHAPTER devoted to subject specialisation must begin by defining precisely what is meant by this term. It may well convey a slightly different meaning to one person or another. This chapter and the following four attempt to outline our views of what a subject specialist does, or is expected to do. Four broad areas are covered in four chapters—'provision', 'exploitation', 'teaching library use', and 'professional awareness'.

But first, to a definition of terms. Guttsman, in an important article entitled 'Subject specialisation in academic libraries', considers that the subject specialist should be responsible for book selection, specialist bibliographical enquiries, giving instruction in a particular subject area to groups of students, classification, but not necessarily cataloguing, which may well be dealt with by a central cataloguing unit, and for certain administrative duties. Holbrook's article on the subject specialist in polytechnic libraries, is, obviously, more precisely relevant to this book, since it is clear that Guttsman's article applies more to university libraries. There are bound to be significant differences between a polytechnic with buildings in Hammersmith and Woolwich, fifteen miles apart, and a new university with one major library in the centre of the campus. Holbrook cites K W Humphreys' simple definition of a subject specialist, — 'a member of the library staff appointed to develop one or more aspects of a library's technical or reference services in a particular subject field.' He goes on in his article to suggest that the subject specialist should organise library services in a particular field, and should be responsible for developing the services, on the one hand, and maximising use, one the other. At least one British polytechnic, Liverpool, is basing its definition and job description very closely on the recommendations of Holbrook's article with a view to future implementation.

It would be fair to say that all the above definitions cover a lot of common ground. Certain areas seem to exist in which it would be suitable for a subject specialist to be involved. It could be maintained that the subject specialist should be responsible for everything to do with his subject, although this is, of course, directly related to the number of subject specialists within the polytechnic in question. Our survey of all thirty polytechnics in Britain showed clearly that there are not enough subject specialists yet; only eight polytechnics of the twenty who returned the questionnaire reported having more than six specialists. This means that, in many cases, a specialist is responsible for three or four related but distinct subject areas, when the ideal would require responsibility for only one or two. Two polytechnics, Leeds and North London, had more than ten specialists, but even our fifteen specialists cover nearly thirty subject areas between them.

If a specialist covered everything to do with his subject, this would presumably involve him in the following activities: — book selection and acquisitions; cataloguing and classification; current awareness and selective dissemination of information services; library instruction; professional awareness, by which I mean the activities of a specialist designed to keep him up to date in his subject area. This might include the writing of a chapter such as this, or the production of a questionnaire to evaluate the spread of subject specialisation within British polytechnics.

The broad areas of 'provision', 'exploitation', 'teaching library use' and 'professional awareness', will be treated in turn by four different subject specialists, all employed in the humanities faculty of the Polytechnic of North London. But before embarking on these chapters, we felt it was essential to establish how 'typical' the scheme of subject specialisation at our polytechnic was, compared with other polytechnic libraries. Obviously, we all had a basic conception of what the job involved, from discussion amongst ourselves and the other specialists in our polytechnic and from our individual job descriptions and experience in the post. Thus, we were able to give our impressions of the function of a subject specialist within the developed systems and structure of one polytechnic. What we needed to find out was to what extent the situation at the Polytechnic of North London was comparable with or indeed applicable to, any or all of the other twenty nine polytechnics in Britain. I compiled a fairly brief one page questionnaire, which was sent to the chief librarian of each polytechnic, including our own. This questionnaire was in three parts: — 1) a section to be completed by the chief librarian, giving brief details of the polytechnic's staff numbers and student population; 2) a section detailing each of the areas relevant to the duties of a subject specialist—book selection, book ordering, cataloguing, classification, current awareness (books), current awareness (periodicals), current awareness (other), teaching library use, attendance at department or board of studies meetings, and attendance at external courses or conferences; 3) a section giving some indication of non-subject duties undertaken by subject specialists, including supervision, information desk staffing, and non-professional duties such as shelving and counter duty.

Unfortunately, only nineteen polytechnics out of thirty returned our questionnaire. It was disappointing that returns were not higher. We had hoped that a one page questionnaire with a four week deadline would not have been considered too much of an imposition. The eleven missing returns could, of course, mean that all my figures and comparisons are falsely biased. However, it seems that the analysis of the other nineteen reveals a very consistent pattern indeed. Details of a twentieth polytechnic were subsequently obtained by interview, and this gave a two thirds return which can be regarded as providing a reasonably representative picture.

Findings of the survey

The twenty polytechnics had 114 subject specialists, who between them, were responsible for a grand total of 183 subjects in forty-eight broad or narrow areas. Statistically speaking, this can be taken to mean that, on average, each specialist covered $1\frac{1}{2}$ subject areas, which is very close to the ideal of 'one man, one subject'. No one covered more than five areas, though the five were, in fact, often widely spread, *eg*, accounting, law, industrial relations, marketing and sociology; or arts, languages, catering, general studies and design. Of the forty-eight different specialisations, areas covered ranged from the general, *ie*, 'everything except science and technology', to the very specific areas covered at one polytechnic. The most popular specialisation was 'Art and design', a post held in thirteen of the eighteen polytechnics which have subject specialists.

Some polytechnics again held the majority of posts. Eight of the eighteen polytechnics had more than half of the subject specialists, — eighty eight out of 163. **Table 1** shows the different subject areas covered by each polytechnic. **Table 2** shows the total number of specialists in each area, while **Table 3** shows the areas of subject responsibility.

107

Subject	Bristol	City of London	Hatfield	Kingston	Leeds	Leicester	Manchester	Newcastle	N E London	North London	Oxford	Plymouth	Portsmouth	Sheffield	Sunderland	Teesside	Thames	Wolverhampton
Accountancy	O			●							O						●	
Architecture				O					●	●	●			●			●	
Art and design	O	●		O	O	O	O	O			●			●	O	O		O
Biology		●	O								●	O			O	●		
Business Studies	●	●	O	●			●				●	●			O	●	●	●
Chemistry		●	O	●							O				O	●		
Cinema and Photography				O														
Community Studies							●											
Computing	●		O	●						●					O			
Construction	●									●								
Earth Sciences		O																
Economics	●			●						●							●	●
Education			O	O					O	O				O				
Engineering	●		O	O	●			●		●					O	O	●	
English								●		●		●					●	
Food Science					●					●		●						
Geography					●					O		●					●	
Geology										●								
Government		O		●														
History					●					●		●					●	
Humanities	O					●				●					O			O
Industrial Relations																	●	
Law	O	O		O						O							●	●
Liberal Studies								O										
Librarianship										O								
Life Sciences				●										O				
Management	●			●		O	●	O		●		●		O	O			
Marketing																	●	
Materials Science																	●	
Mathematics	●	●		●						●						●	●	
Metallurgy		O														O		
Modern Languages	O	●		●						O	●	O		O			●	
Nursing and Welfare							O											
Philosophy											●						●	
Physics		●												O			O	
Planning	●				O			●		●							●	
Politics						●												
Polymer Science											O							
Psychology		●	●	●														
Science	●						●	●			●	●		O				●
Social Administration				●														
Social Sciences	O	●			O	●								O	O			●
Social Studies								●		O	●				O			
Sociology		●								O							●	
Surveying								●			●						●	
Technology			O		●		O	●				●						●
Telecommunications										●								
Transport		O										O						

Table 1: Subject areas covered.

1	Art and Design	13		25	Physics	3
2	Business Studies	10		26	Psychology	3
3	Engineering	9		27	Sociology	3
4	Management	9		28	Surveying	3
5	Modern Languages	8		29	Construction	2
6	Science	7		30	Government	2
7	Social Science	7		31	Life Sciences	2
8	Architecture	6		32	Metallurgy	2
9	Biology	6		33	Philosophy	2
10	Chemistry	6		34	Politics	2
11	Law	6		35	Transport	2
12	Mathematics	6		36	Cinema and Photography	1
13	Technology	6		37	Community Studies	1
14	Computing	5		38	Earth Sciences	1
15	Economics	5		39	Geology	1
16	Education	5		40	Industrial Relations	1
17	Humanities	5		41	Liberal Studies	1
18	Accountancy	4		42	Librarianship	1
19	Geography	4		43	Marketing	1
20	History	4		44	Materials Science	1
21	Planning	4		45	Nursing and Welfare	1
22	Social Studies	4		46	Polymer Science	1
23	English	3		47	Social Administration	1
24	Food Sciences	3		48	Telecommunications	1
						183

Table 2: Relative popularity of subject areas of a total of eighteen polytechnics.

	Bristol	City of London	Hatfield	Kingston	Leeds	Leicester	Manchester	Newcastle	N E London	North London	Oxford	Plymouth	Portsmouth	Sheffield	Sunderland	Teesside	Thames	Wolverhampton
● Applies to <u>all</u> subject specialists																		
○ Applies to <u>some</u> subject specialists																		
Book selection	●	●	●	●	●	●	●	●	●	●	●	●	●	●	●	○	○	●
Book ordering	●	●							●	●	●		○			●	●	●
Cataloguing	●			●					●	○	●				●		●	●
Classification	●			●					●	●	●	●	●		●	●	●	●
Current awareness (books)	●	●	●	●	●			●	●	●	●	●	●		●		○	●
Current awareness (periodicals)	○	●	●	●	●			●	●	●	○	○	○		●		○	○
Current awareness (other)	○								○					●			○	○
Teaching library use	○	●	●	●	●	●	●	●	●	●	●	●	○	●	●	●	○	●
Attendance at dept meetings	○	●	●	●	○			●		○	●	○	●	●	●			●
Attendance at conferences	○	○	●		○	○	●	●		○	●	●	○		●		○	○
Non subject specialist duties	●	●	●	●	●	●	●	●	●	●	●	●	●	●	●	●	●	●

Table 3: Areas of subject responsibility.

I would suggest that this table could be interpreted in two ways. By reading along, it is possible (for example) to deduce that 'book selection' is regarded as a necessary responsibility for *all* subject specialists in all polytechnics except Thames and Teesside; and even these two have some specialists who do subject book selection. Also it is clear that non-subject duties take up a proportion of all subject specialists' time. By reading down, it is possible to tell two things; from the number of black dots against each polytechnic, how uniformly subject duties apply to *all* subject areas; and from the total of white and black dots, how fully each polytechnic interprets the range of subject specialist duties.

It will be seen from the above tables that the Polytechnic of North London, with fifteen subject specialists, is closest to the ideal of 'one man, one subject'. It is also more than a mere coincidence that all the areas listed in our questionnaire as being possible subject specialist duties— book selection, book ordering, cataloguing, classification, current awareness, teaching library use, attendance at departmental meetings, and attendance at relevant conferences—appear in most of our job descriptions. Obviously, in a system covering six sites, all geographically separated, and with fifteen subject specialists, uniformity of approach is difficult to obtain. Furthermore, some areas of study lend themselves more readily to instruction in library use than others. The individual motivation of the particular subject specialist, too, will determine the priorities he or she gives to different parts of the job. Each subject specialist will view his department in a slightly different way, and the service provided should not only be carefully tailored to suit the existing needs of the department, but should also cater for future developments.

It would be fair to say that no two of our subject specialists give exactly the same weighting to different parts of their work. This is currently being investigated by Pauline Thomas of Aslib with the help of the North London staff. Equally, no one subject specialist could hope to cover adequately every part of the job description, which is, after all, an ideal—based on limitless time, facilities, opportunities and materials. In the real work situation, other activities of a supervisory or purely non-professional nature take up a proportion of one's time, and consequently reduce the time available for fulfilling the pure subject specialisation duties.

Yet, in spite of the fact that each subject specialist does his or her job differently, there is a fair degree of overlap and uniformity within our polytechnic, particularly in the production of a current contents list in most subject areas. Termly meetings of all subject specialist staff, usually devoted to a specific topic, *eg*, tape slide subject guides, or cataloguing and classification in subject areas, help to ensure that each member of staff is aware of the services provided by the others. Ideas exchanged during these sessions frequently lead to further experimentation and the adoption of new techniques around the system. Senior coordinating staff are part to play a part in this activity, particularly when a local idea is seen to have a wider potential.

111

CHAPTER VII

Book selection

Keith Davis

IT IS NOT the intention here to provide a description of the mechanics of book selection, acquisition and exploitation, as this has been done satisfactorily by others. Instead, it is hoped to emphasise services to the user, whether he belongs to the academic staff or the student body. The aim will be to discuss the problems involved in the selection of materials and their acquisition. Consideration will also be given to the tasks of providing information on book selection designed to assist academic staff, of choosing a supplier, and of the difficulties of achieving adequate bibliographical control of varying types of material.

Acquisition of materials is based on selection procedures which, in turn, rely on the adequate provision of information designed to guide the selection decision. It is a prime task of the subject librarian to keep his academics well informed about materials appearing in their subject areas whatever the physical form of presentation. The selection of bookstock is a fundamental part of the work of the subject specialist in that he is in an ideal position to bring together subject knowledge and bibliographical expertise. This combination allows for skilled stock selection for a particular course, when conjoined with a deep understanding of user needs resulting from close liaison with academic colleagues.

Selection can be current and retrospective, the former being based on a multitude of reviewing organs, published lists and the usual plethora of book news arriving with every mail. Retrospective purchasing can only take place in the light of detailed consultation and the various processes of stock editing. Selection may then occur via the examination of subject bibliographies, desiderata lists, existing external collections and use of the second-hand sources.

In setting up the policy for book selection, particularly in establishments such as polytechnics, which have experienced major changes in size and function, a number of problems have to be considered. The subject librarian might well be faced with questions such as: 1 What information is required to guide selection? 2 How is information best obtained? 3 What methods exist for presenting the information to others? 4 Who is the information for? 5 How much time can be spent on selection? 6 Who is to instigate selection and who is to have the final control?

Answers to these questions are intimately tied to the role of the subject librarian and his ability to perform certain tasks satisfactorily. The confidence of academic staff in the librarian cannot be assumed, particularly in a situation where previously the library has offered only limited services and facilities. The appointment of a new subject specialist librarian, offering for the first time a service in depth to a department, will not necessarily be wholeheartedly welcomed, particularly when shared decision-making comes into operation. Whenever the library takes a more positive and active stance, this can lead to misunderstandings and a measure of resistance from those conditioned by past practice. Fortunately, experience at North London Polytechnic suggests that the majority of academic staff are only too delighted to accept this greater level of library activity and involvement in processes having direct bearing on teaching efficiency and student satisfaction.

To discover what information staff require, the subject librarian must see them individually and construct personal profiles based on teaching and research interests. This personal approach is the essence of the subject librarian's work and cannot be stressed too highly. Contact can be made formally through staff meetings and in committee or can be achieved quite informally as circumstances allow. Whatever approach is used, it is important for the subject specialist to be recognised as a colleague offering specialist skills and an understanding of the work of the department. In the first instance, the initiative may have to be taken by the librarian who should gradually create a close relationship with academic colleagues by dint of persistence and a real level of efficiency. The provision of a high quality service to the individual lecturer is probably the key to acceptance.

The gathering of information of benefit to the individual involves careful scrutiny of newspapers and journals, both general and specific, as these contain advertisements, book reviews, literature surveys and books received features. Trade papers and all kinds of publishers' information provide another rich source of book news. Additionally, the subject librarian will make contact with other specialist librarians and will be aware of the resources in other institutions, through visits to libraries, attendance at conferences, earlier working experience and the reading of professional literature. The exchange of current awareness bulletins, accessions lists and other specialist publications is common practice in the profession and is another valuable source of selection information.

Once the librarian has gathered his information, he must decide how to present it to academic staff. An individual notification service, based on cards containing basic bibliographical information may be used. This has the advantage of presenting highly selective information to the individual, based on his profile. A more wholesale approach is that of circulating publishers' lists and similar publications to the staff of a department. This has the advantage of allowing the lecturer to look at a wide field of material so that he can decide what is of interest to him. On the other hand, the circulation of lists around a department presents problems of control and time lag, and may well duplicate items already sent direct to lecturers, who are frequently swamped with material issued by publishing houses.

In providing such a service, it should be remembered that information about books is not in itself sufficient to meet the needs of staff. A large proportion of the most interesting material appears in periodical form. A copy of an article, or notification of the author, title and source, can be sent to the individual when it is known that the subject is of intense interest. However, if the aim is to satisfy the needs of a department, the most comprehensive and convenient vehicle for this purpose is the specialist current awareness bulletin. This should be produced at regular intervals and distributed to each member of staff in the department. It may well contain lists of new books and other information, but should devote considerable space to the contents pages of current journals. The pace of academic life is such that many staff find it increasingly difficult to keep in touch with journal output and can benefit greatly from the quick perusal of some well-chosen contents pages. The current awareness service requires the backing of efficient photocopying and request services. Furthermore, it can have considerable impact on the efficient creation of specialist off-print collections.

It is appropriate to warn that the response to such services will not be evenly enthusiastic. Information cards will not be returned, circulating lists will stick at an untraceable point, and some current awareness bulletins will be despatched to waste paper baskets. Genuine forgetfulness, a certain lack of interest and sheer pressure of work will create a lack of response and will lead to some wastage of effort on the part of the librarian. However, experience shows that academic staff are largely appreciative of this kind of service, which results in an exchange of views on selection and the making of wise decisions particularly when financial restrictions are rather pressing. The lack of interest in stock selection or a measure of over-eagerness to buy everything in sight on the part of a few academics are problems which have to be handled delicately by the librarian. He may ultimately have to fill gaps and maintain a balanced stock, to counter lack of interest and to control excesses of zeal, but his first task is to make sure that academic staff have before them the necessary information associated with the efficient selection of stock.

It should also be remembered that student needs should influence book selection. The subject specialist will have a broad understanding of these needs through his involvement with academic staff, but some aspects of selection will be influenced by direct contact with students. Conversations at the information desk and discussions during courses of library instruction will provide some guidance to the librarian of the special requirements arising from essay writing, problem solving and project work. Decisions concerning not only selection of titles, but also of numbers of copies required, and how these are to be organised, will frequently determine the level of student satisfaction with the library. It may be necessary to establish special counter collections of material, sometimes on a short-term basis, designed to meet specific study needs. Exceptionally heavy demand for a relatively small number of titles over a limited period can influence book selection disproportionately.

Once the information guiding book selection has been made available, we come to the important question of who makes the selection decision. It is a truism to say that most library operations are centred on the stock the library holds. The selection of material is, therefore, of paramount importance. Priorities must be established based on subject expertise, teaching, learning and research needs, and all these related to library finance. The assistance and participation of those using the library is essential if the subject librarian and the expertise of the academic staff must be joined in effective action. Many polytechnics and universities have teams of subject specialist librarians, operating at departmental or faculty level, who are deeply involved in stock selection which is seen essentially as a joint venture with academic colleagues This guarantees that the selection is of a high quality and ensures that the librarian becomes adequately involved in departmental or faculty matters related to library services and operations. A thoroughly organised, cooperative effort in book selection inevitably involves the librarian in discussions concerning course content, teaching methods and student needs.

Cooperation of this sort inevitably raises problems which can only be resolved in individual ways in particular settings and circumstances. The librarian must be aware of the need to maintain a balance in selection, and must strive to encourage the less enthusiastic lecturer to take a greater interest in library affairs, while restraining the ardent bibliophile who tends to unbalance the selection for a department in his eagerness to build up his own area of bookstock. Similarly, the librarian whose over confidence leads him to think that he alone can decide on the ideal stock is working under a grave misapprehension. Stringent financial controls make it essential that librarians and academic colleagues work together on book selection. The lecturer will greatly influence the choice of stock for course studies, and the librarian has a particular responsibility to maintain a balance and plan for the longer term.

Once a department has gained confidence in the ability of the librarian, its staff will be prepared to leave a great deal of the selection to him. This will be the case particularly when financing is generous and the academics are hard pressed with other duties. Lecturing staff in the polytechnics not only carry the normal teaching duties, but are also frequently involved in heavy administrative responsibilities, a seemingly endless round of committee and teaching group meetings, and, with the decline of external courses and the creation of new CNAA degrees, are fully engaged in course planning and academic change. When a department's staff are relatively free of such commitments and where money is scarce, then book selection is likely to come under closer scrutiny. An inevitable offshoot of course planning will be the attendant re-examination of the library's bookstock in the appropriate areas. The CNAA subject boards look critically at the stock before a new degree course is launched and the introduction of an entirely new discipline can lead to the rapid spending of several thousands of pounds on new bookstock. The provisional list of books will be produced jointly by all the specialist teachers involved in the course and will be strengthened by the additions and suggestions of the library staff who, in any case, will be asked to carry out a substantial programme of bibliographical checking before final lists are submitted.

The acquisition of materials

Thus far, I have been concerned to point out the advantages of the subject approach as opposed to the more traditional functional type of library organisation. The development of personal, user oriented services inevitably brings into question the relationship of this aspect of the work with that of the technical services. While the breakaway from the strictly functional approach to librarianship has been welcomed in the polytechnics, nevertheless, the reader contact side of the work inevitably relies heavily on the efficiency of the support services. Holbrook sees four main roles for the subject librarian: policy maker, educator, academic and manager. It is in the latter area that the mechanics of book selection, acquisition, processing and indexing are placed. If selection is the key to the quality of a library collection, then acquisition and its effective organisation becomes of vital importance in that it directly affects the quality of the service the subject specialist can offer. Long delay in the acquiring of material or ineffective use of booksellers can seriously undermine the realisation of the more sophisticated service aim.

The concept of the subject specialist operating a highly personalised service to one or two departments is bound to create a certain conflict of interests, given that there is an increasing trend towards the centralisation of library management, including book acquisitions, in the face of rising costs and the search for maximum efficiency. The independence of the subject librarian and his freedom to deal with academics can work against the trend towards central servicing. However, these two aspects of service are not incompatible, if a proper division is made between technical processes and user services, and as long as a clear policy and overall guidance emanates from a central management team devoted to the creation of a homogeneous service. The task of the central team is to coordinate the activities of the subject specialists, to offer guidance and assistance in overcoming problems, and to advise on appropriate methods and techniques, without creating a rigid pattern of activity at the departmental service level. The guidelines set by the central team should allow the subject specialist to experiment and test new ideas with the department, and to then submit the benefits of this experience to the scrutiny of group discussion, with the object of bringing about refined and improved concepts of service.

Literature on the subject of acquisition work is not abundant and the young subject specialist may find he has to make his own, often painful, way during his first appointment, particularly in the situation where a central acquisition unit, staffed by experienced bibliographers, is not available. In this situation, each subject librarian becomes directly responsible for selection and acquisition of materials.

The normal pattern of book ordering is well understood, but within the context of orders placed with a reliable bookseller, there are a number of possible pitfalls. Routine acquisition procedures are not always appropriate depending on the nature of the materials to be obtained. In order to obtain the fullest range of stock, in all its physical forms, the subject librarian will have to deal with disparate suppliers, both the book trade proper and with a vast range of specialist bodies and institutions not normally thought of as suppliers of books. These include professional organisations, municipal authorities and obscure organisations often difficult to trace and who operate systems of book supply which do not fit conveniently into the normal patterns.

The choice of a bookseller will involve such practical considerations as the convenience of location, the range and level of material of his stock, the speed of delivery and the range of processing services offered. A bookshop having a good range of bibliographical tools, and a manager of a helpful disposition and an understanding of academic needs should be able to offer a good service, but account will also have to be taken of discount arrangements and service charges, items which can lead to the saving of hundreds of pounds in a financial year.

The subject specialist, sometimes advised by academic colleagues familiar with the book world related to their teaching areas, is in a position to study the pros and cons of the situation and to place his orders accordingly. Where a central unit exists, its striving for economies of scale may place the staff of the unit in conflict with the specialist, who will be more concerned with using the best supplier for particular groups of material. However, the central management of the library should be able to effect a suitable compromise between the two elements. Broadly, the bulk of orders will be placed with a few large booksellers offering a full range of services and capable of making frequent deliveries. This will not rule out use being made of the small specialist supplier, such as a foreign language bookshop or a non-print media publisher.

Neither centralised nor localised acquisition work avoids problems associated with the establishing of standard routines, work flow, the answering of queries as to progress, and the dealing with urgent requests. The ability to provide such refinements has crucial bearing on the quality of service to be offered by the subject specialist, who is often under pressure from academic colleagues to produce urgently needed items. It is, therefore, imperative that the subject specialist receives the backing of a first rate unit which is as equally concerned with micro decisions and localised efficiency as well as the construction of a major book ordering system perhaps coping with fifteen to twenty thousand items each year.

Certain classes of material will present problems of acquisition, whatever system is used. Foreign language publications demand the use of specialist suppliers, and it may be necessary to use a direct overseas contact in order to obtain the fullest range of stock. Specialist lecturers in this field can frequently make direct contacts for the library during the course of study visits. Out of print material also presents difficulties in that the inception of new courses and the appointment of academic staff frequently creates a demand for materials which the library does not possess and which are no longer available through normal bookselling channels. The search for out of print items is often most fruitfully pursued on a subject basis through a specialist second hand supplier. An investigation of such possibilities is best carried out by the subject specialist librarian who can then advise his central unit on likely sources.

Microforms and other non-print media present problems in that they suffer from loose bibliographical organisation and a wide range of suppliers, many of whom are difficult to trace. At North London, the appointment of a media resources librarian has provided a necessary guiding influence of great benefit to the team of subject specialists. Regular consultation between the media librarian and the specialists ensures that vital items are not missed and that appropriate purchasing channels are used. Between them, the staff are able to sort their way through the somewhat chaotic world of non-print material. Where the subject specialist has no backing from a media organiser, the responsibility for selection and acquisition will largely rest on his shoulders as it is unlikely that academic staff will have the time or the interest to carry out such work. It is correct that this should be so in the sense that any subject specialist operating today should extend his interest to appropriate materials in whatever physical form they are published.

Exploitation of stock
Once the stock has been acquired, the remaining task facing the subject specialist is of how best to exploit fully the range of material available.

The beginnings of effective use are linked with the apposite classification and cataloguing of the bookstock. The careful selection of entries and the subtle choice of subject headings can contribute a great deal to the exploitation of material. Subject specialists should act as catalogue advisers and play an active part in the allocation of classification numbers and the creation of a detailed subject index. A total involvement in the cataloguing of all materials is probably not a good thing in that this will involve the specialist in many hours of backroom activity and could seriously interfere with his programme of reader contact. However, it is equally the case that his advice and help with the more severe classification problems should ensure sensible placings based on the bias and needs of the patterns of study in a particular faculty or department. Once more, we are faced with a compromise between the benefits of a totally functional approach using centralised technical services and the advantages to be gained from the use of experience gained at the local level.

New material, once ready for the shelves, can benefit first from display in a new book section. This will be for a short time only and some libraries display such stock in an easily supervised area at or near the issue desk and do not allow the books to be issued for the period of a week or so. This results in many of the books being reserved before they reach their normal places on the shelves.

The subject specialist may also like to arrange small subject displays of material within his area of the library. This can bring together old and new stock related to specific interests or study needs of students and can collect in one place material in various physical forms when these may be shelved separately under normal circumstances. Books, pamphlets, oversize material, offprints, tapes and the like can be brought together for a week to demonstrate the breadth of stock available.

Given that the bulk of material is filed in sequence around a large library, another pertinent aspect of exploitation is that of adequate guiding. R P Carey of Hatfield Polytechnic did a great deal of work in this field, and, as a result, several institutions have looked more closely into the matter. Certainly, a library which is confusingly arranged and lacking in guidance reduces the impact of its stock, which may be perfectly adequate but badly presented to users. The library will need some general guiding designed to lead the user to the appropriate main area. Once there, more specific guiding will come into play. Whether it is well judged and appropriate will depend a good deal on the interest of the subject librarian, who should be prepared to devote thought and effort to the guiding of his own section, within the context of the house style and general requirements.

Printed guides are another means of exploiting stock. The general library guide has been widely used in the academic sector, but, as is demonstrated elsewhere, not with sufficient care. Library publications of all kinds have tended to suffer from inadequate preparation, and the limp, duplicated library guide has too often been the main offering of the library service. A good quality guide, as produced by Hatfield or North London, or information sheets housed in an attractive folder, such as those offered by City of London, can help the student find his way around the library. If these are supplemented by more specific publications, prepared ideally by the subject specialist, they can be of great assistance, particularly to first year students. During a typical year, the specialist will be able to produce a series of short guides aimed at very specific groups. Some will be used to support the teaching programme, taking the form of seminar handouts, while others will receive distribution at the issue desk. It is worth remembering that students are given a mass of paper information when they begin new courses. It is, therefore, all the more essential for printed library publicity to be of a high standard and genuinely geared to student needs.

The librarian can also maintain an attractive noticeboard on which to display current information. Displays of book jackets and items of current awareness value can be placed in the heart of the building where they can conveniently be perused by students. While general lists of acquisitions can be exceedingly dull, we have found that short, specialist or sectionalised lists are well used by staff and students in a department. Publications aimed at a relatively small number of students on a particular course are frequently well received. This specialist, personalised approach increases the use of material and helps to persuade users that the library is genuinely concerned to meet their needs.

The availability of the subject specialist at an information desk located conveniently near his stock encourages the student to present his requests and enquiries. It is noticeable that students will be more prepared to use this service after receiving some basic instruction from the subject specialist in the classroom situation. This points to the essential inter-relationship between library publicity, programmes of instruction and individual help in the library. The whole should be viewed as a programme designed to cultivate the users' understanding of the library and its services.

The subject librarian will constantly monitor user needs and will involve himself in the planning of circulation and reservation systems designed to maximise the use of bookstock. Exploitation of existing materials will depend on the close cooperation of the librarian and his academic colleagues, who can jointly decide which items are in demand and for what periods. Heavy demand on sections of the bookstock should, ideally, be anticipated during the course of the liaison between the department and the library. Additional stock can be purchased to meet pressures, but, bearing in mind financial limitations on multiple copies, it will be necessary to construct sophisticated systems for categories of material to be issued to the reader on a special basis. Items in heavy demand will have to be placed in short loan collections which allow for four hour or one day periods of loan. A book containing a key chapter or an offprint of particular value can be read in the library by at least a dozen students during the course of a week, given that the item is temporarily placed in the four hour loan collection. This arrangement will clearly be affected by teaching patterns, which tend to create heavy, localised and short term demands. It is imperative, therefore, that the librarian be given sufficient information to enable him to anticipate demand and to return the item to its normal location as soon as possible. Where a special counter or undergraduate collection is built up, it is essential for the team of subject specialists to edit the stock not less than once each session. Otherwise, it will grow to a vast size and will effectively hide books from the eye of the reader, who might otherwise discover valuable material during periods of shelf browsing. It is essential, therefore, to have an issue system capable of accommodating these different categories, including the non-book media, one which is responsive to change when demands alter.

Throughout this section, the importance of good liaison between the academic and the librarian has been stressed. The existence of a cooperative spirit and a desire for mutual help should guarantee wise book selection and the subsequent thorough exploitation of resources. The efficacy of the selection and exploitation activities of the subject specialist will depend a great deal on his ability to make substantial contact with the staff and students of his department.

CHAPTER VIII

Information services for academic staff

Philippa Dolphin

FEATURES OF SPECIAL LIBRARIANSHIP such as the provision of SDI and current awareness bulletins have been slow to spread to the academic sector. In his paper published in 1962, R S Smith, librarian of Nottingham University, claimed 'information dissemination, which I have suggested is the really distinctive feature of special librarianship, with its production of bulletins and abstracts, seems to have only small application in the academic library'. Since then, there has been a growing acceptance that there is a place in the academic library for some kind of information service. Even the most primitive information service may do much to promote library use and create good relations with academic staff. A good service by a specialist who is aware of the research interests of the academic staff in his department can save a great deal of time for lecturers who are attempting to cope with both the information explosion and a great increase in student numbers. In view of the limited resources available in polytechnic libraries, anything but the widest possible exploitation of material can be very wasteful. Finally, it has become apparent that unless librarians play a more active part in the dissemination of information, academic staff are likely to begin establishing their own departmental information services. Once the confidence barrier has been overcome, a central library based information service run by subject specialists is far more likely to be efficient than a proliferation of independent services. In fact, information services are a logical extension of existing recognised library functions such as reference work and teaching, and, as Maurice Line points out in his 1972 paper on 'Information services in university libraries', if information personnel were established in university departments then libraries would lose not only their information activity, but they might also lose much of their teaching function, since provision of information and the instruction in the use of information sources are closely related.

The types of information services given by subject specialists will naturally vary a great deal according to the subject area, the number of academic staff involved and their attitudes, and the physical relation of the library to the department. In certain subject areas, particularly in the sciences, a fairly good current awareness service may already be provided by an external publication such as *Current contents—life sciences* or *Chemical titles*. No one service is ever sufficient, however, and it is essential that the subject specialist should publicise all the current awareness journals received by the library and encourage the fullest possible use of these often rather expensive tools. Scientists are generally more accustomed to using current awareness and information services than researchers in the social sciences or humanities, although such services are less likely to be appreciated in an academic context than in an industrial situation where the competitive and commercial attitude of researchers produces a keener interest in what other researchers are doing. Fortunately, many of the scientists in polytechnics have come from industry and may be more receptive towards special library style services.

The fact that scientists may already be served by an external current awareness service does not mean that there is no room for a subject specialist librarian in that field. There is always a need for retrospective searching of the literature, information about library accessions, and a good informal information service. In fact, it is very important that external services should not be allowed to replace this personal service by library staff, as Maurice Line has shown in his paper 'Summing up: the information service in practice', three of the most important aspects of a good information service are that it should be personal and informal, day to day and flexible.

Compared with scientists, workers in the social sciences and humanities are poorly served by the external current awareness services. The volume of literature, particularly in the humanities, is far less, and keeping up to date is not of such importance to the humanities researcher. The experimental information service provided for social scientists at the University of Bath between 1969 and 1971 has shown, however, that many social scientists do have unsatisfied information needs and react very favourably to a personalised information service. These findings are borne out by the experience of librarians in the Polytechnic of North London library in Highbury, which covers the social sciences. Members of the sociology and law departments all make very good use of their subject specialists, and the appointment of these subject librarians has stimulated interest in library matters and encouraged academics to entrust bibliographical queries and problems to library staff.

A survey like the Bath experiment has yet to be carried out to ascertain the latent information needs of academics in the humanities, despite a call in the Parry report on academic libraries for an investigation to assess the precise demands for information services amongst university lecturers. Our experience so far at the Polytechnic of North London has shown that there are very distinct information needs in the arts departments, though these vary greatly according to the discipline. Amongst the lecturers who use the polytechnic arts and humanities library, the desire to keep up to date with recent research is probably greatest in the education and geography departments. Lecturers in the education department also appear to be the most persistent in asking for retrospective searching into various topics. Geographers are more interested in access to specific factual information such as statistical data or details of recent developments such as North Sea oil exploration or the new local authorities. The least enthusiasm for our current awareness and accessions bulletins is to be found in the language and literature department. It is difficult to ascertain how much this is due to the nature of the subjects and how much to the absence of any tradition of use of information services in these disciplines. Members of staff are showing a good deal of interest in a card service informing them of new books published in their subject areas and this generates a large number of book orders. Our subject specialists in these areas feel there is much they could do for the arts researcher in the way of retrospective searches and current awareness, but this requires a gradual change of attitude amongst the academic staff, involving a greater confidence in library staff and less reliance on the old tradition of self help.

Information for postgraduates and students

Naturally, the subject specialist will not confine his information services to academic staff alone. Postgraduates are provided with current awareness bulletins and are encouraged to make use of the services of their subject specialist. On the whole, their demands on the library service tend to be restricted to heavy use of interlibrary loan facilities. They are working in very narrow fields and do not generally regard library information services as being of much potential value to them. Increased library instruction to postgraduates could do much to alter this state of affairs. If it were possible for subject specialists to demonstrate to each intending postgraduate exactly how to conduct a thorough literature search, research students would tend to have more confidence in their subject specialists and the services they offer. Similarly, undergraduates engaged in projects and essays will often require assistance in literature searching and the location of specific items of information. They may also wish to browse through the library produced current awareness bulletins, which should be available for consultation in the library. Again, good library instruction will serve to increase confidence in the library service. A library notice board in each department can also be a useful way of advertising library services. Details of library activities and pockets containing library publications can be attached. Academic staff can do much to help the library in its provision of services to students by warning in advance of new topics to be studied, special options and student projects. This enables the subject specialist to look out for material on these topics, to make up special files of newspaper cuttings and to compile bibliographies for students. Obviously, students cannot be provided with the same kind of information service given to staff, but a friendly and helpful attitude on the part of the subject specialist can greatly improve the library's image and encourage greater use and confidence amongst students.

Current awareness
The main type of formal information service which is undertaken in the Polytechnic's arts library in Kentish Town is the production of current awareness bulletins for each department. Eight different bulletins or accessions lists are produced at regular intervals, either monthly or fortnightly: *Current contents in English, classics and linguistics, Teaching studies current awareness bulletin, School practice and media accessions lists, Current contents in geography, Current contents in history and philosophy* and three versions of *Current contents in modern languages*, for the French, Spanish and German departments. Every member of staff in each department receives a copy, and extra copies are produced for notice boards, the library and for staff in other departments or branches of the polytechnic with overlapping subject interests. The geography current awareness bulletin, for example, is also sent to the geographers on the teaching studies staff, and to the library at Holloway

Road, where it might be of interest to the town planners or geologists. In split site polytechnics where similar or overlapping courses are taught in different branches, any device which publicises relevant library materials held at other branches is very useful, to librarians and academics alike. The bulletins comprise photocopied contents pages of current journals, together with photocopies of the author catalogue cards of recent accessions. When the journals arrive each morning, the periodicals assistants photocopy the contents pages and pass these copies and the journals on to the relevant subject specialist who keeps the copy of the contents page for his bulletin and scans the journal for news and reviews before putting it out for the readers. Often a journal may be scanned by more than one specialist, and its contents page appear in different bulletins. *Local historian*, for example, is seen by the geography and the history librarians. Bulletins of this kind are particularly effective if the specialist scans a large number of fringe journals which the academic researcher would not normally have time to see. The contents pages of these fringe journals will occasionally appear in the bulletins whenever they contain relevant articles. Cooperation between subject specialists is particularly important here, since they can pass on to each other details of interesting papers in different journals. The modern languages specialist, for example, may come across various articles in languages journals which might well be included in the philosophy bulletin. Unlike external awareness services, these bulletins are highly flexible and can be changed as courses and research interests vary. This is of particular relevance for today's polytechnics where the traditional style of University of London degree courses are gradually being replaced by CNAA courses of a more applied and interdisciplinary nature. Another advantage of this type of service which is very important in a busy polytechnic library, is that production of sufficient numbers of one issue of a bulletin takes little more than one hour of staff time. Although the photocopied catalogue cards do tend to look a little unprofessional, this is a very quick method of publicising accessions and is essential where typing time is at a premium.

Future developments with regard to current awareness bulletins are now under consideration. It is hoped to produce joint bulletins from two or more of the site libraries covering a particular subject field. These lists would be suited to the needs of interdisciplinary courses, and would hopefully encourage readers to exploit the resources of libraries on other sites. The establishment of a central book ordering and cataloguing unit in the near future should facilitate the production of these joint subject oriented bulletins.

Current awareness services have been welcomed in most quarters, though they have received some unfavourable criticism. The main criticisms tend to be that people should do their own searching and that they do not have time to peruse bulletins. The view that researchers should look at current periodicals for themselves is obviously valid, particularly in small well defined subject fields. In many cases, however, researchers are likely to find relevant articles in thirty or more journals received by the library, and since it is not practical to circulate journals to academic staff, the bulletin seems the most effective method of helping staff to keep abreast of current periodical literature. Certainly there is no other way of informing staff of new book material received by the library, unless they are given to regular browsing in the class catalogue. The second criticism is often made and is particularly disturbing. Staff who have no time to read a current awareness bulletin must have no time for any periodical literature, which, considering the soaring costs of periodicals and binding, raises serious questions as to the appropriate level of provision. Careful thought should also be given to the physical production of the bulletins. They should be both readable and economical of materials. A recognisably standard cover in a good house style and brief easily read contents are necessary features of a well designed bulletin. Double sided copying, reduced on the Rank-Xerox 7000, in our experience, combines the merits of economical use of paper with reasonable clarity of presentation. Each bulletin is not normally more than ten pages long, and since these modest publications greatly stimulate the use of the current journals collection, they can be said to make a significant contribution to the programme of library exploitation.

A second and more personalised current awareness service in operation at the polytechnic is the provision of references either on cards or in the form of photocopies of abstracts or sometimes of the whole article. This type of service is obviously much more time consuming than the production of current awareness bulletins, and owing to the pressure of work on the subject specialist, it tends to be restricted to the more interested and appreciative members of the academic staff. It is hoped that when more staff and time become available in the future, it might be possible to provide a better service to some of the less library oriented lecturers. To some extent, this service overlaps with the production of current awareness bulletins, but it has certain advantages in that it is more flexible, more personalised and more immediate. If, for example, a journal from a related subject field is found to contain an article relevant to one lecturer in a department, it may be preferable to notify him by card or by sending a photocopy of the abstract than to include the entire contents page in the bulletin. This supplementary service, therefore, enables a slight reduction in the size of the bulletin and makes it easier to scan. Occasionally a journal paper may have an uninformative or misleading title which may mean that it is unlikely to be picked up from a current contents bulletin; in such cases, it is preferable to send a photocopy of the abstract, first page or whole article to a lecturer who might be interested. Being more personal than the current awareness bulletin, the card service is less likely to be ignored. Also the cards are easily filed away in a personal index for future reference. Lastly, the SDI on cards has the advantage of being speedier than the bulletin which appears once a fortnight.

Although the dissemination of current awareness bulletins does not necessarily require the services of a subject specialist, this more personal and informal type of service obviously does. The subject specialist must have a good knowledge of the interests of his staff, both in lecturing and research. Some familiarity with the subject is also essential in order to understand the terminology and to gain the confidence of the staff. In his paper on 'Information services in university libraries', J.Hall states that 'organisation on subject lines is probably the greatest asset of a library attempting to establish information services'. Informal liaison with lecturing staff over lunch and coffee is one of the most effective ways of keeping up to date with their research interests as well as with different developments within the department. The Bath experiment showed that researchers who were in close daily contact with the information officers received a better service than the researchers at Bristol University to whom it was extended, which emphasises the importance of being close to one's clients and having a 'personal familiarity' with their research needs.

The uniqueness and topicality of the local current awareness service must occasionally give way to the convenience of the purchased information service. The assessment of information needs at the Polytechnic of North London showed that a significant number of the administration and directorate were interested in some form of higher education information service. The task of providing a local one was considered wasteful in the light of the cheapness and reliability of the service in this field prepared by Aston University. All heads of department and senior members of the administration are given copies of this bulletin and, for the moment, they are happy to accept it as a useful additional source of information. Hatfield Polytechnic also issues a bulletin on higher and further education, which is circulated throughout the Hertis organisation, and, for many years, industrial and educational personnel have benefitted from the multi-topic current awareness service on cards pioneered by Gordon Wright and his staff. Our own fortnightly current awareness bulletin on library science literature, originally designed to meet the needs of the teaching and research staff of the school of librarianship, is now circulated to the professional library staff throughout the polytechnic. Outside interest in this publication has now developed to the point that half the output is sent to other libraries and institutions, both in the United Kingdom and overseas. These examples suggest that services originally produced to serve local need may have wider application, and there seems to be some potential here for wider circulation and cooperative production. The danger inherent in such developments is that ambition begins to ride too high, and the advantages of cheapness and speed of production become lost in the pursuit of other objectives.

Other services

A similar service to the sending out of cards is the dissemination of publishers' blurbs, booksellers' catalogues and PICS cards.

Where book selection is done largely by the subject specialist, this sort of material tends to be sent out only where he is uncertain of the value of the publication. Photocopies and cards are also sent out to notify academics of interesting book reviews. Notification of recently reviewed books seems to be particularly appreciated in the language and literature department. One of the subject specialists for this department circulates bulletins comprising photocopied PICS cards and library notification cards. Lecturers tick any item they would like added to stock, whilst the specialist concerned keeps a pile of the cards he has photocopied, in order to ensure that the department is not notified more than once of the same book.

A fair amount of retrospective searching is done by the subject specialists for various members of staff, although we have tended not to advertise this service too much because it can be very time consuming. These searches are normally for staff engaging in some new research, or compiling student reading lists. Occasionally searches are done when staff request that holdings in certain subject areas be improved. Sometimes it is necessary to encourage a member of staff to do his own literature search by showing him the different bibliographies and suggesting various search terms. In fact, one of the greatest problems of the subject specialist is having to strike a balance between encouraging staff to recognise and use the services he has to offer, and discouraging certain members of staff who expect long bibliographies to be prepared at a day's notice. The Bath Experimental Information Service to social scientists showed that academics rated retrospective information services more highly than the circulation of contents pages. Evans and Line suggest that the higher cost of this service must be taken into account when planning an information service, since one search may take several hours and cost as much as £10. A very important quality for the subject specialist is, therefore, the ability to be diplomatic when dealing with demands for retrospective searching. In some cases, it has been possible to produce printed library bibliographies on important topics of current interest, such as the raising of the school leaving age and the various government white papers on education. These save a lot of time for both staff and students and are very popular.

It is hoped, in time, to produce more guides to literature for staff and students in order to encourage them to do their own retrospective searching. Our social sciences library has produced a guide to indexes, abstracts, bibliographies and government publications in the social sciences, as well as other pamphlets such as *Introductory notes on the law collection.* These are available to students, and packages of relevant guides are sent to all new lecturers joining the polytechnic staff. Other guides and information sheets being produced include general library guides, subject periodicals lists and lists of specialist booksellers and libraries in London.

Another service which takes up a great deal of the subject specialist's time is the provision of a general reference service to his department. The subject specialists take it in turn to man the information desk, but there is a strong tendency for members of the academic staff and even students with routine non-subject enquiries to seek out their own subject specialist rather than ask the person on the information desk. This means that the subject specialist is frequently disturbed by queries which could easily be dealt with at the information desk where the relevant bibliographies and quick reference works are to hand. Any specialised subject queries are generally referred to the relevant librarian. Wherever possible, the subject specialist's desk is located as near as possible to the literature of his subject, so that the education librarian sits in the school practice and media room, the modern languages librarian in the German and Spanish room and so on. This accessibility helps tremendously, and, provided the subject specialist looks approachable, students will come with a variety of queries which they would otherwise be unwilling to present. Personality is particularly important in this type of library work since students are easily discouraged by an offhand manner.

It is evident that an information service of any kind does serve to increase demands on the library, and since the introduction of subject specialists into the library at Kentish Town, the pressures on clerical staff running the reservations and interlibrary loans systems have greatly increased, although this is also partly due to the programmes of library instruction given to students. A sufficient number of good clerical staff must be available in order to relieve the specialist of routine library tasks and to cope with this increased demand on library services. As Peter Woodhead points out in his article on subject specialisation in three British university libraries, the subject specialist system tends to break down when specialists become overburdened with routine or administrative work. Job dissatisfaction will, consequently, increase and the amount of time spent actually helping readers may decrease drastically. Not unnaturally, academics are unlikely to be willing to entrust complicated subject queries to someone whom they regularly see shelving books, manning the issue counter or filing the issue. Nor are they likely to disturb someone who is constantly hidden away cataloguing piles of books. Similarly, though a large amount of routine duties may restrict the information activities of the subject specialist, there may also be problems if he attempts to provide a good information service, neglecting his other library tasks. It is hoped that the establishment of central book purchasing and cataloguing units and perhaps the later introduction of automated systems to cope with routine library functions, will enable library staff to devote more time to the reader. Another development already under way in the sciences is the introduction of computer based information retrieval systems. Rather than replacing the subject specialist, these are likely to strengthen the case for library staff with good subject knowledge able to cope with the special input problems associated with this type of service.

Whilst many other services in academic libraries can be measured and tested, information services are very difficult to evaluate. With time, it may be possible to build some measure of feedback into the information services at the polytechnic, but where so much of the service is personal and informal, this will not always be possible. Maurice Line's argument that a library with a limited stock and well developed information services may be giving better service than the one with a much larger stock and minimal services, is particularly relevant to polytechnic libraries. Resources in polytechnics are still limited compared with those in universities, despite recent big increases in book funds, and a good information service can help compensate for these inadequacies.

CHAPTER IX

Planning library instruction

Barbara Penney

THERE ARE MANY advantages in having the subject specialists responsible for library instruction, not least because of their intimate knowledge of the literature available and their involvement in the book selection designed to meet the special needs of courses. Their attendance at boards of studies and teaching group meetings gives them a substantial understanding of course content and teaching and examining methods employed in a particular area. If library instruction is to be relevant, then all these factors have to be borne in mind. The lecturer's confidence in the library staff tends to be passed on to students, a factor which Patricia Knapp found to be vital to the success of instruction programmes at Montieth College, Wayne State University, Detroit. If teaching staff feel that library instruction is vital, then they will be quite willing to cooperate with the time tabling of this work. A great deal of the ground work with academic colleagues can be carried out quite informally in staff common rooms and over lunch time discussions. This is often the best method in the early stages, rather than the more formal approach through the head of a department. The whole question of library instruction is best raised informally and first spoken of as a natural offshoot of other library activities as the occasion arises.

Job descriptions for the subject specialists at the Polytechnic of North London stress the importance of a total involvement with appropriate departments. This involves the creation of teaching programmes based on the defined needs of students attending particular courses. In a large polytechnic, the team of subject specialists available are able to assist each other in the preparation of their teaching, and to join together in group teaching activity when the need arises. The additional help of a senior coordinating librarian undoubtedly encourages the less experienced to overcome organisational and other difficulties. This has worked well at North London in that the Library Education Officer has been able to negotiate with departments showing a preliminary interest in courses, and has been able to give advice to the subject specialists on teaching methods, content and presentation.

Time tabling remains one of the most persistent problems associated with programmes of library instruction. The difficulty of fitting additional items into an already crowded timetable tends to hamper progress. At Reading University when library instruction was first introduced, students were expected to attend after lectures and on Saturday mornings. The resultant lack of attendance need not have surprised anyone. Library instruction must be given at convenient times and the librarian should be prepared to offer flexibility of timing and approach. However, it is important that while maintaining reasonable pliancy, the library staff should not undertake instruction at such short notice as to prevent satisfactory preparation. The adequate presentation of library instruction may well govern the amount to be asked for in the future, and academic colleagues should realise the importance of careful preparation when library programmes are being negotiated.

While many teachers will be happy to hand over a group for library instruction and look forward to a free period, it is often useful to persuade them to join the students during the session. His attending will encourage student involvement and his appreciation of the value of what the library can offer will tend to encourage interest among his students. He may well be brought into discussions during the session and be able to introduce examples of his own use of library materials and services to supplement those instanced by the librarian. Very importantly, it is also possible that the lecturer himself will absorb a great deal of useful information about the library as he listens to the library talk. It is more than likely that his understanding of bibliographical sources, indexing services, abstracts and other publications will be increased as a result of his attending.

A further problem associated with timetabling is whether or not the sessions should be compulsory. Given that no lectures in the department are obligatory then it would be impossible to impose this ruling for the single occasion. If attendance is voluntary then it must be assumed that only a proportion of the students will attend. Therefore, it is important to see that the importance of the library sessions is stressed, and that academic colleagues are prepared to put their weight and influence behind them. Hopefully, one assumes that there will be only initial reluctance on the part of the student to attend library instruction. Once the teaching is seen to be valuable and relevant, then the level of attendance will be maintained.

In devising a programme of library instruction it is important to give appropriate attention to the needs of specific students. The rapid dispensing of a standard talk, or the total reliance on a tape slide programme, is not sufficient. The wide diversity of courses in the polytechnics, ranging from the professional to the traditional academic, in itself demands a whole range of approaches. Students of librarianship, teaching or applied social studies require library courses different in kind and content from those provided for students of an academic discipline, such as history or philosophy. This is best illustrated by examining the library instruction offered to students of teaching studies at North London Polytechnic.

Library instruction for students of education
Students studying to be teachers are faced with an amazing diversity of interests. They need to be aware of sources in the main field of education and in their choice of academic option, whatever that may happen to be. Their involvement in periods of teaching practice must also be allowed for in presenting library courses. Each of these areas involves different preparation in terms of level, content and approach. Over the period of a three year course the student of chemistry can easily come to know of a few basic aids, such as *Chemical abstracts*, but for the student of education the problem can be somewhat more complex. He must become familiar with the range of bibliographical tools servicing education, and also those in his academic area, particularly if he is expected to present some form of dissertation.

An education department of a polytechnic cannot hope to maintain first rate collections for all optional subjects, but there is a reasonable chance that the appropriate disciplines will be provided somewhere in the college for the benefit of students in other departments. This should enable the student of education to gain access to a substantial collection of material and to benefit from the help of a second subject specialist well versed in the literature of his discipline. Such a situation also provides opportunity for joint teaching programmes in which the teaching studies librarian provides the understanding of the needs of the trainee teacher, while the discipline specialist is able to offer the benefit of his subject knowledge.

The teaching practice element in the work of the student of education is again unique in the demands it makes on the library. During the sessions of library instruction it must be borne in mind that students are interested in tools as much by level as well as by subject. A single topic can be considered at the infant, junior or secondary level. Teaching methods, especially in the primary school, are such as to draw on all aspects of a theme, for example 'the seashore', and to investigate this first through obvious links such as shells, sand and water, and then to seek further associations within music, art and children's literature. Library instruction, therefore, must demonstrate the possibilities of this approach and should present to students the full range of resources to be used when the thematic method is employed. This, incidentally, presents a substantial opportunity to make use of not only books and journals but also the illustrations collection, wallcharts, slides, tapes and gramophone records. Assuming the library has developed such services, this type of library instruction presents an excellent opportunity for a thorough-going multi media approach. The student will have his imagination stirred by the linked thematic approach to his subject and will also be taught how to handle the equipment and software of the nonprint media.

Work with other categories of user

For students reading a joint honours degree, there will be a need for at least two sessions of library instruction covering the bibliographical tools of each area. Where a dissertation is called for, then a more detailed knowledge of the tools of research will be required. Students on a modular course should benefit from a library session devoted to the presentation of material associated with each of the modules. Furthermore, experience at the Polytechnic of North London suggests that students undertaking course assessed work generally require more assistance with literature searches than those involved in examined courses. The elevated importance of essays for course assessed work leads the student to supplement tutor's reading lists with his own searchings. This automatically involves the librarian to a greater extent and underlines the importance of the use of adequate search technique in the preparation of written work.

Researchers and lecturers involved in part time research make heavy demands on the library service and can benefit from library instruction geared to the appropriate level. Several polytechnics have organised for postgraduate students programmes covering appropriate bibliographical sources and also offering guidance in correct bibliographical citation and the organisation of material. At this level, the library tutorial is effective, but small group work should not be ruled out. A minority of research staff will be disdainful of such guidance, but experience at North London suggests that most young researchers are more than happy to receive help and advice from the librarian.

Content of courses
Library instruction can be tailored to most needs. Traditionally, academic libraries have offered a printed library guide, a quick talk on basic services and a guided tour of the library. This package is often part of a hectic induction programme held in the first week of term. How much of this is retained is highly questionable. If this is the only library instruction offered to students it is unlikely to match the needs of the typical undergraduate, and, in any case, presented as it is, too briefly and too soon, it is likely to lack relevance. It is only when the student begins to grapple with essays and reading lists that the details of how to use the catalogue, overnight loans, offprint collections and the like will become of real importance. It is essential to give this kind of information to all students but at a time when it relates to need. To be realistic, it is quite clear that the timing of induction courses raises administrative problems which conflict with ideal timing from the educational point of view. The sensible solution is to arrange discussions with department or faculty with a view to planning alternative timing and the possible recourse to more varied methods of instruction.

In the first session of library instruction certain constraints govern content and method. At the beginning of the academic year the whole library is busy dealing with the influx of hundreds of students. Time is short for small group work or individual guidance. In this situation, the librarian must accept the problem of talking to large numbers and must be prepared to lecture to a whole course. Alternatively, use can be made of the several media presentations of the library, involving the use of tape slide guides or videotape and film. The employment of repeating tape-slide, suitably located in or nearby the library has much to commend it as an initial introduction to services, but it is important in these early days to introduce the subject specialist to the students who are to study in his area.

Many librarians feel a need to explain to new students the intricacies of the catalogue and the classification scheme. Personally, I feel that the barest essentials of the classification scheme are necessary. The student needs to be aware of the main classes and to have some understanding of subject order, but it is all too easy to lapse into detail only of interest to the librarian. The student, however, does require a reasonable understanding of the catalogue as this can make the difference between tracing a book or not. While it would be stressed that students can seek help in locating material, there is some value in explaining matters such as headings for government publications, entries for Open University material and other types of publication requiring complex entry. It is when giving this type of theoretical information to students that accompanying practical work is useful. Information is reinforced when the students have the theory backed up in a practical way. The exercises should avoid the over simple as these will be of limited value and will not test the students skill sufficiently. Examples necessitating the use of all sections of the catalogue should be used, and the student, once having received adequate instruction, should be presented with problems designed to test his understanding of how best to approach the catalogue *ie*, to discover whether to use the subject index, the subject catalogue or the author sequence. If the problems set help the searcher to discover the significance of headings, series titles, class number and accession number, then this can be of practical value within a very short time. If books about an author are filed after the works by the author, then this information should be brought out in examples used.

This kind of library instruction can only work for the small group, and students should not be over exposed to catalogue instruction. The use of teaching sets and tape-slide guides could usefully supplement exercises requiring the use of the actual catalogue. The latter can easily cause congestion and annoyance, and tends to create problems of supervision and control. But work involving the use of the catalogue thoroughly tests the students' understanding and tends to highlight the practical difficulties to be faced.

As the students progress in their courses, they will need to know more about the bibliography of their subjects. In the first year, the coverage can be relatively simple, as the students will not be involved in project or dissertation work. Their attention should be drawn to a few of the more obvious bibliographical sources and some time should be spent in introducing the full significance of the book in all its parts, with examples drawn from well chosen items carrying a substantial measure of subject interest. To illustrate points with positive examples, rather than talk about hypothetical cases, is invariably more effective.

Students at this level also need to understand the particular value of periodicals. Aspects such as topicality, specificity, and their ability to carry argument and counter-argument should be stressed, as should the existence of different categories of journal—the practical, popular, learned or research orientated. At this stage, too, it is advisable to introduce the basic indexing and abstracting services covering the journals in the appropriate subject areas. Periodical articles and offprints can be of enormous value to groups of students having to write an essay on the same topic, and many undergraduates need to be introduced to the key journals and the various indexing tools if they are to gain access to the necessary information.

By the time students recieve further library instruction they will have used the library a good deal and will have become aware of the usual frusstrations of insufficients multiple copies and the book which is always out. Therefore, it will be useful for them to have information about interlibrary lending, the request service and the various specialisation schemes. It is very useful, for instance, for the students reading philosophy at North London to know of the fine collection of material housed at the Swiss Cottage library. Directories of local public libraries, listing schemes of specialisation, and reference tools describing services of interest to students could be introduced at this stage.

It is also appropriate in the early days to present to students the value of the specialist encyclopedia and dictionary. This class of material is useful when the student is examining a topic for the first time. *The International encyclopaedia of social sciences* and the *Encyclopaedia of philosophy* offer valuable introductory material together with substantial if occasionally dated, reading lists. Works such as the *Dictionary of national biography* and the McGraw *Encyclopaedia of science and technology* are heavily used once known, but it is often left to the librarian to introduce these to students.

The question of how to present material deserves careful thought. As most of the students will be studying within a particular discipline, such as geography, it is preferable to present bibliographical information on this basis rather than in general terms. Furthermore, as there is so much literature available in any one discipline, it is often helpful to plan a literature search within one particular area of that discipline. For example, a search centred on pollution could be of value to geography students, and it would be stressed that, although a pertinent topic had been selected, the essence of the exercise was the understanding of the technique of literature searching. During the course of this work with students it would be possible to reinforce earlier teaching on the use of the catalogue and other library tools and services without appearing to repeat information given in the former sessions.

Later it may be desirable to introduce a literature search relevant to each student's needs. In Hazel Mews' chapters of case studies in her book *Reader instruction in colleges and universities* it was noticeable that in preparing examples for student use she invariably consulted with academic staff to ensure that suitable topics were selected. In some cases the lecturer chose a topic about which the student knew something, but it was just as   that a selected subject would be one to be covered in the near future. Both choices would seem to be justified in that each guaranteed a sense of involvement with material of direct interest to the student.

When students embark on dissertations or projects they require further help with sources. Instruction should build on earlier efforts and should be offered to the individual or, possibly, to the small group. Those involved in this type of teaching find that interest is at a high level, possibly because the student is faced for the first time with the task of searching out a substantial amount of related material which he has to organise carefully and present systematically. Therefore, the techniques of literature searching need to be reinforced and developed, with students being reminded of broader and narrower terms, correct methods of citation and modes of presentation.

At this stage the student will benefit from a quick revision of the use of the major bibliographical works, but will find particular value in the specialist indexing and abstracting services such as *Geo abstracts, British education index,* ASLIB's *Index to theses* and NFER's current *Researches in education and education psychology.* Work with these aids will bring to the attention of the student the importance of conference papers, research reports, and other less easily traced material, with which to supplement books and journal articles.

In the educational field, apart from individual research being carried out, there are a number of organisations engaged in research having substantial practical value of particular interest to the polytechnic student. An example of this is the Schools Council's involvement in research into curriculum subjects, with the aim or providing new ideas and material for use in the classroom. Organisations such as these are often willing to talk to students interested in these research areas.

Another aspect of library instruction which needs to be covered at this advanced stage is the actual organisation of the material gathered. The need to accurately record specific references and place these in some card index system is worth stressing for students, who frequently tend to forget essential details and fail to note the origin of material they wish to use. The failure to note exact page references and details of author and title, frequently cause the student to waste hours of precious time. The card index offers great flexibility and can be used to note details of where a work was consulted, whether or not it was borrowed on inter library loan, and whether it was out of print and difficult to obtain, as well as for recording all the basic detail normally supplied in a bibliographical reference.

Methods of instruction

As stressed earlier, methods of instruction should be tailored to fit the content, as far as possible, but other constraints influence the planning of a programme of library instruction. These include the numbers of students in involved, the time allocated for a course, and the resources available to back up the teaching. The existence of a good reprographic department or a well equipped media resources unit, will exercise a great influence on how the teaching is carried out. Printed handouts, tape slide programmes, tapes and video tapes can influence how, when and where the programmes are conducted.

Media programmes of instruction seem to be very popular at the moment in educational libraries. Most of the efforts can be described as experimental and research is being carried out at Surrey University, sponsored by the Media Sub-Committee of SCONUL, to evaluate tape-slide presentations. The results of these labours will be made available, and should lead to a better understanding of content and use of equipment. Apart from their novelty, media programmes have certain advantages over the lecture method. This is particularly noticeable during introductory sessions when large numbers of students recieve basic information within a short space of time. The programmes can be prepared during the quieter periods of the year and can be used to avoid repetitive talks by hard pressed library staff at the beginning of sessions. They also allow the large visual presentation of detail from catalogue cards or the printed page which would be difficult to present in any other way in the large scale teaching situation. The preparation of the more ambitious filmed introduction to the library involves much greater cost and problems of professionalism in the acting. The short film produced by Central Office of Information on Hatfield Polytechnic Library and the film introducing public library service produced by the Open University have proved to be excellent teaching aids, but home produced efforts have been less satisfactory. The acting ability of librarians tends to be limited, while professional assistance with production and acting can be very costly. The rapid dating of this type of presentation suggests that there is much to be said for a cheap tape slide presentatation which can be easily edited and revised. These programmes should not lack personal content and should be backed up by distribution of printed guides and the holding of question and answer sessions, whenever possible.

Media presentations can also be employed for more advanced and detailed instruction. Experiments at North London suggest that programmes outlining the literature of a subject or explaining the rudiments of a literature searching can be usefully presented to either groups of students or to individuals using the Surrey carrel. A programme illustrating the literature of law has had a measure of success. Bibliographically this subject is very demanding and the complexities of the sequences of law reports and statutes are not easy to present. However, it was found possible to summarise a great deal in a tape-slide programme of fifteen–twenty minutes duration, and this has been used successfully with undergraduates reading law.

A recent survey of self instruction using tape slide guides at Newcastle Polytechnic discovered that students preferred private study to group instruction. Fewer in the self instruction group thought the tape slide elementary and a significant proportion claimed more confidence in using the library and were better able to retain the information imparted. However, isolated study can lead to organisational and supervisory problems and removes the possible benefit of contact with the library staff and the exchange of views in the group.

Assuming the student has received initial instruction by means of a talk and guided tour, or the use of introductory tape slide programme, or possibly a combination of these methods, how next to proceed is problematical. But if facilities are available and staff time can be spared there is a good deal to be said for seminar instruction, which experience shows to be time consuming but effective. By working in small groups, the students can gain easy access to the bibliographical material under discussion and can study informally and at the right pace. Individual problems can be diagnosed and solutions found. The knowledge the student gains of the librarian who is likely to be his subject adviser over the three year course, will encourage him to present queries in the library and will form the foundation of a highly personal service. Furthermore, it is possible to organise highly specific seminars, such as 'The language difficulties of West Indian children in a multiracial classroom', which would be wholly inappropriate either as a main lecture topic or as a subject for a tape slide presentation. Seminar work can usefully be supplemented by collections of material, possibly prepared in the form of a wall display, and by the provision of carefully prepared printed handouts.

Individual instruction, or the tutorial, has much to commend it. The proper functioning of this system may depend on careful planning and an advance booking system. This is of particular value to the final year student who is about to prepare his dissertation. Jacques Hayward, at Hatfield, has been particularly successful in developing this kind of activity. However, it is very time consuming and must be placed in the context of all the other duties facing the subject specialist. The availability of such a service should be made known to students, but it should be left to them to approach the librarian for help. A substantial number will take advantage of the system and will tend the produce better dissertations as a result of these sessions. Ideally, the student will receive help from his personal tutor and from the subject specialist librarian. Discussions will cover the precise area of work to be done and will not lapse into a general survey of search technique, something the student should have covered at an earlier date.

An important aspect of library instruction which is often overlooked or under rated is that arising out of a simple enquiry at the information desk. Even if the question presented appears to be a simple one, perhaps involving the classification number of a particular subject, it often pays to probe a little deeper into the actual requirements of the student. Such an approach could elicit fairly complex needs which might necessitate the use of the catalogue and various bibliographical aids. It could also present the librarian with the opportunity of commenting on the literature known to him and lead to a deeper evaluation of the problem on the part of the student. Frank Hatt, when librarian at Canterbury College of Art, thought this the most worthwhile type of instruction, as it was obviously relevant to the student at that moment, and therefore all the more likely to be absorbed.

Assessing the value of library instruction

Many librarians giving library instruction find it difficult to evaluate. Follow-up exercises involve a good deal of work and, in any case, have to be examined, corrected and commented on. Hazel Mews developed a system at Reading University involving the use of bibliographical tools, and written answers to set problems. The students' answers were discussed at the beginning of the following seminar. The subjects given during these sessions were selected in close cooperation with academic staff and entailed first, the use of general reference books and textbooks, and, second, the searching of relevant periodicals, indexes and abstracts. The development of a search from the unknown produced lively discussion and no little student ingenuity. The students were able to learn a lot from other's experiences of literature searching during the follow-up discussion sessions, but Hazel Mews comments on the substantial investment of time on the part of the librarian in preparing these exercises.

At Hatfield the emphasis is on the integration of library instruction with the normal work of the student. Jacques Hayward bases the practical library work on the projects already being undertaken by students as part of their academic work. The projects are assessed both for academic content and in terms of bibliographical skill. The correctness of bibliographical citation and the quality of literature searching employed both influence the student's grading. This approach automatically includes a check on the efficacy of library instruction, which may have involved initial group work followed by at least one or possibly several private tutorials. Whatever system is used, it is advisable for the librarian to attempt some kind of check on the student's understanding. Library instruction is a practical art, open to experiment, and easy to adapt. It is important, therefore, to obtain feedback from students to guide the refining of courses.

The aims of library instruction in polytechnics concern the acquainting of students with the staff of the library, its resources and how best to make use of them. One of the most important elements is that of making the library staff known to the student user. In a survey carried out by Southampton University, after the introduction of library seminars in 1965, it was reported that as time went on an increasing percentage of students, classed the library staff as always helpful. Experience in Hertfordshire and at North London fortifies the view that contact through library instruction invariably leads to a greater willingness on the part of students to approach the librarian for advice. It has been found at North London that the policy of having subject specialist information desks adjacent to the appropriate bookstock has reinforced the image presented at library instruction seminars. Students come to know their librarians and are quick to make use of services.

Seminar instruction also leads to an increase in the purposeful use of the catalogues, and it has been noted that students become more precise and coherent in presenting their questions to library staff. They also become more adventurous in their use of material other than books. Bibliographies and periodicals and their indexes are consulted more frequently and the non-print media is used more heavily. There is also an undoubted increase in the use of the request service, inter library loans and special collections. However, it is interesting to note that Patricia Knapp discovered that while library instruction improved the student's ability to use services, it did not necessarily improve the student's motivation to make wider use of the library. She claimed that the way in which students used resources was dependent, above all else, on the lecturers' attitude towards the library and methods of study. This again illustrates the importance of good liaison between the library staff and academic colleagues, and suggests that the maximisation of library resources will only result in a situation where lecturer and librarian share objectives.

It appears that to achieve great effectiveness library instruction should form an integral part of courses of study. Content should be adapted to the needs of students on particular courses, and the form and timing of presentation should be carefully considered. Subject specialist librarians are particularly well placed to realise the needs of those reading a discipline. Library instruction should help a student be at ease in his library and to enjoy a wider programme of reading. His newly acquired skills should help him with his essay writing and should certainly be a major factor in the successful preparation of his dissertation.

The typical student should complete his course having had access to books, journals and other media, sufficient to meet his reasonable demands, and he should at the end have learned how to use a library and its services effectively. This is as much part of his education as anything else he may experience and could represent the finest possible investment of his time in preparing for further private study or research activities.

CHAPTER X

Professional awareness

Martin Walker

OF THE FOUR broad areas—provision, exploitation, teaching library use and professional awareness—into which the duties of a subject specialist fall, the first three have already been treated. The fourth 'professional awareness' I take to embrace four distinct areas: a) literature scanning, b) representation, c) liaison, d) contact.

I am in no way suggesting that any of the above areas are the exclusive preserve of the subject specialist. However, I think that, in a fully developed system of subject specialisation where a librarian is totally responsible for one subject, then professional awareness is of the greatest importance, and must be developed and maintained as the job expands. The areas listed above, therefore, become an integral part of the concientious subject specialist's own 'awareness'.

Literature scanning
This is obviously an area in which most librarians are already active; certainly the subject specialist has no sole prerogative. His reading is, however, likely to be rather more intensive than that of a librarian less involved with one restricted subject area. General weekly periodicals, like the *Economist, New statesman, New society, Listener* and *Spectator* are all quite useful for book reviews, as are the quality Sunday newspapers, which also often include helpful general literary articles. Other publications of a more bibliographical nature, such as *BNB, British book news* and the *Bookseller* are also essential reading.

For the subject specialist, a vitally important area for literature scanning will be periodicals of subject interest to his or her particular subject field. There will be a significant number of periodicals in the library's holdings likely to be of direct value both to the subject specialist and the lecturer. Their value will be firstly as a source for authoritative reviews of new works in a particular subject area. In my own case, I produce from subject periodicals and other publications a termly list of *Recently reviewed books* for staff in modern languages. The second use of subject periodicals is for the location of useful articles of particular interest to courses or options, or indeed relevant to the lecturers' individual research. It is a reasonably simple process to take a photocopy of the contents page and reviews from each relevant periodical issue, and to compile from this a regular current contents list.

Additionally, in a subject like modern languages, which is my own area of activity, there are a number of general periodicals which give an insight into the life and customs of other countries. I consider it important at least to skim through periodicals like *Paris-match, Der Spiegel, Blanco y negro, Cuadernos para el diálogo* and *DDR revue* for general news, as well as *Nouvelles littéraires, Insula* and *die Zeit* for book reviews.

Publishers' catalogues are also a fruitful source for locating possible acquisitions; again, in modern languages, for example, a large number of overseas publishers and booksellers provide booklists and bibliographies. Secondhand lists are also very useful, as are the catalogues from the major British publishing groups, for helping to fill gaps in subject stock.

Being 'well-read' and up to date in subject terms is, I feel, very necessary preparation for any subject specialist; doubly so as literature scanning is a direct preparation for current awareness services, and also facilitates book selection and ordering, as well as keeping the librarian in touch with general developments in his subject areas.

Representation

This area immediately raises the problem of acceptance. Whereas literature scanning can be seen mainly as a librarian's task rather than a lecturer's, it may well be felt in some quarters that librarians should not be represented at the various levels of committee and sub-committee, departmental meetings, faculty boards and course committees, in which polytechnics seem to abound. However, it is fairly common for one librarian to be invited to attend departmental boards of studies. It would be most satisfactory if subject specialists were always to attend these meetings so as to be able to advise in library terms on the subjects for which they are responsible. If the subject specialist is competent at his job, he will feel able to sit on the board by right, not merely because of his subject knowledge, but also, more especially, because of his library and librarianship knowledge. He will be capable of advising the department on the likely difficulties in acquiring certain overseas materials, warning of possible delays in orders, commenting on the strength and weaknesses of bookstock in a precise area, or advising on the acquisition of audiovisual materials where relevant. The subject specialist should be able to contribute on any matter relating to library provision, exploitation or instruction in his subject. It is also to be hoped that the subject specialist will have gained sufficient acceptance within his department to be consulted in his own right as a 'subject literate' member of the staff with something valid to contribute to discussion.

Even more important than boards of studies will the the question of the introduction of a new course. It must be hoped that the subject specialist will be invited to contribute to this most important area. This is particularly necessary in interdisciplinary courses. For example, a course in Latin American studies will include not only Latin American language and literature, but economics, history, geography, culture and institutions. It is absolutely essential that the subject specialist be involved from the very beginning in all discussions relating to the introduction of any such course.

Liaison

Liaison is an area of the subject specialist's duties which is perhaps more difficult to carry out successfully than most others; for whereas literature scanning depends to a large extent on the specialist's bibliographical ability in selecting relevant books or articles, liaison depends almost entirely on the two psychological factors of 'acceptance' and the mix of individual personalities. The subject specialist's own personality is of paramount importance, since individuals not possessing a naturally outgoing nature may well find making contact with colleagues one of the more difficult aspects of the work.

Another possible source of difficulty in this area is the extent to which individual lecturing staff are 'library oriented' or 'library conscious'. Particularly in a polytechnic where subject specialisation has only been developed over a relatively recent period of time, lecturing staff may be more accustomed to having to find their own information, and may, therefore, have problems adjusting to the 'luxury' of a subject specialist in their subject area. Alternatively, some lecturers may have had little or no dealings with the library on a direct basis in the past. The presence of a subject specialist may persuade them to take a more active role in exploiting the library, instead of leaving it to their colleagues; unfortunately, it may also give rise to a basic mistrust.

Acceptance, therefore, is most important, and the subject specialist must be capable of convincing staff that he is sufficiently well versed in his subject for an exchange of ideas to take place at a more or less equal level. Incidentally, the crucial impact of the situation where library staff are on administrative grades, and are consequently regarded as not being academic staff, is beyond the scope of the present discussion. It is, nevertheless, of some significance, as the librarian on academic scales may have a much better chance of being treated as a member of the academic staff by the lecturer.

If the subject specialist can point to higher research in his subject field, or at least a first degree in one or more of his subject areas, this too should help to establish his position with lecturers, many of whom will have an MA or PhD in the same subject field. Librarianship qualifications will, inevitably, not carry as much weight in the mind of a lecturer, but it will be expected that librarians are 'qualified'. On the other hand, a demonstrable bibliographical expertise, a real enthusiasm for the subject and an ability to communicate, will tend to overcome difficulties of a technical nature.

What are the ways in which liaison with one's lecturers can be put to mutual good use? I think the most important way will be in using the lecturers' more specialised knowledge in specific areas, not just the ones in which they are actually engaged in teaching, but their research interests too where applicable. The exchange of information need not be entirely one sided—the librarian, for his part, will be well placed to advise on the acquisition of particular publications, drawing upon his extensive bibliographical knowledge.

Informal discussions with lecturing staff at every possible opportunity will also be mutually beneficial. Again, the subject specialist starts at a distinct advantage, in that he will be in touch with the whole spread of his subject area. He can more easily spot neglected areas of the bookstock, which may be directly attributable to a previous lecturer's lack of interest in library provision. The librarian can usefully and unobtrusively fill out such areas to achieve a more balanced bookstock. The individual lecturer, for example, may be rather more concerned with the library's holdings on classical French drama, and have little interest in the French postwar novel which may be beginning to feature increasingly in the teaching of the department.

The ideal situation will, of course, be one of reciprocity. The lecturer should, whenever possible, be made aware that the personal approach of the librarian is devoted to his own subject. In other words, the library, while providing an overall service, is personalised to a great extent within this general framework. It may take a year or so before the lecturing staff all realise and accept that the library, and in particular the subject specialist, has a valid contribution to make. But once that acceptance is gained, fruitful results can quickly come from sensible cooperation. In the last resort, success or failure of such ventures will stem directly from the extent to which the librarian is prepared to go more than half way to meet the lecturers to whom he is responsible.

Contact

Following a logical sequence of provision, exploitation and teaching, the subject specialist can build up his services to a certain extent through his own ideas and those of his colleagues. But it is clearly not enough to view one's job in the context of one polytechnic or college. It was for this reason that we decided to conduct our survey of subject specialisation in polytechnic libraries. It is for the same reason that the subject specialist should endeavour at all times to learn from the advice and experience of others in his field.

In a polytechnic built on several separate sites, or even several buildings on one site, the first step towards this will already have been taken, as subject specialists will hopefully have compared notes with their colleagues. Each subject specialist's job is, as I have said, dependent on such variables as the librarian's own personality and experience, the attitude of his lecturer, and the extent to which an ideal job description can be met within the constraints of staff, finance and time. Despite this, a large degree of similarity does exist in the work of subject specialists, as reported in the questionnaire.

My own position may be of some interest here. I was appointed as the last of five subject specialists in one building, and as the thirteenth of a projected total of at least fifteen, now reached. This meant, of course, that I was able to pick up a lot of useful hints from the services offered by the existing subject specialists. From this starting point, I was able to go on and develop my own services within a broadly established framework of similarity. This process was significantly aided by the holding of regular group meetings of subject specialists. Above all, these meetings ensured a reasonable degree of similarity in current awareness services which benefited from the adoption of a recognisable 'house style'. They also encouraged formal and informal discussion and criticism of each other's work. The occasional presence of a contributor from another polytechnic helped to generate new approaches to selected areas of activity. This also prevented attitudes becoming too insular and complacent.

Exchanges of this kind are convenient to arrange among the five Inner London polytechnics, all of which have some subject specialists. To exchange experiences with your subject twin in another polytechnic is a most useful exercise. Where greater distances are involved, an undertaking such as the questionnaire sent out by our polytechnic usefully establishes common ground, and the pattern of exchanges of correspondence, telephone calls, exchange of publications and gatherings at COPOL conferences all assist the continuing development of professional awareness.

Another vitally important kind of contact must be made with specialist institutions dealing with one's subject area. To use a modern languages example again, Latin American bibliographical needs are admirably covered by the Institute of Latin American Studies of the University of London, but other organisations such as the Hispanic and Lusobrazilian Council are likely to prove useful too, as will the Latin American library at Senate House.

Once again, the personal approach must be fostered, and visits to institutions are likely to pay dividends. But, of course, the only real way to make such contacts is by attending courses and conferences relating to one's subject. This will not only demonstrate the librarian's willingness to learn and derive benefit from the greater experience of other 'specialists' in his field, but also shows that the librarian is sufficiently interested to benefit from the experience of others. New methods and attitudes once aired at a conference, can be adapted to suit the personal requirements of one's own specialisation. This absorbing of ideas is, I feel, quite defensible, since any possible benefits will advance the library's own reputation for being forward looking in its attitudes, and should directly benefit both the requirements of lecturing staff and the services provided for staff and students alike.

In some cases, international visits and conferences will be useful. My own position as a languages subject specialist has undoubtedly been helped by a study tour in 1972 to libraries in Paris, and by attendance as an observer at the General Council of the International Federation of Library Associations in Liverpool in 1971. More recently, I was a member of a small group of librarians who spent two weeks on an exchange visit to Stuttgart, sponsored and organised by the British Council and the International and Comparative Librarianship Group of the Library Association. In this case, the opportunity to observe the workings of German librarianship in city, 'county' and university libraries was of immense value. Being able to talk on equal terms to my German counterparts in both university and 'county' libraries was equally invaluable. I would hope that I returned to my present post with my views considerably broadened. The international exchanges enabled me to form a greatly enhanced view of the possibilities of my post. Although German libraries seem to operate in a rather more constrained context of closed access and a generally conservative attitude towards exploitation of stock, they are after all coping, albeit in a different way, with the same basic situations, needs and requirements.

I have tried in this section to cover the different ways in which I consider 'professional awareness' can be pursued. In short, I would hope that in subject specialisation, perhaps more so than in other less customer-oriented aspected of librarianship, tangible benefits must result from a wider view of one's individual situation. However adequately or successfully one feels the needs of one's clientele are being met, improvements will always come from the greater experience of others. The larger view is essential at all times. It is to be hoped that, in the same way, this chapter may be of some assistance to others interested in the development of subject specialisation.

BIBLIOGRAPHY

W Ashworth 'Administration of diffuse collections' *Aslib proceedings* 24 (5) May 1972 274-83.

F H Ayres 'Case against MARC: how strong is it?' *Library Association record* 73 (7) July 1971 130-31, 142.

D E Bagley 'Libraries in polyrechnics and colleges of technical and further education' in *British librarianship and information science 1966-1970* edited by H A Whatley. (Library Association 1972). 389-396.

T Bristow 'A reading seminar' *Education libraries bulletin* No 32 Summer 1968 1-9.

City of London Polytechnic Library and Learning Resources Service *A diary survey to establish time and cost data for library processes* (City of London Polytechnic, 1973).

N F Clarke 'Library education in an era of media' *Contemporary education* 62 (1) November 1969 61-66.

A Coppin 'The subject specialist on the academic library staff' *Libri* 24 (2) 1974 122-28.

R E Coward 'The capabilities of the British MARC record service in terms of the academic library' in C K Balmforth and N S M Cox *Interface* (Oriel Press, 1971) 126-39.

C A R Crosland *The role in higher education of regional and other technical colleges engaged in advanced work* (Woolwich Speech April 27 1965) (Department of Education and Science Administrative Memorandum No 7/65, DES, 1965).

C A Crossley 'The subject specialist librarian in an academic library: his role and place' *Aslib proceedings* 26 (6) June 1974 236-49.

R M Dougherty 'Paradoxes of library cooperation' *Library journal* 97 (9) May 15 1972 1767-70.

B J Enright *New media and the library in education* (London, Bingley; Hamden, Conn, Linnet Books, 1972).

S M Evans and M B Line 'A personalized service to academic researchers' *Journal of librarianship* 5 (3) July 1973 214-32.

S M Evans 'Information services for the universities' *Aslib proceedings* 25 (12) December 1973 484-90.

R A Fern *Problems and opportunities facing the libraries of the new universities* (Unpublished diploma study, Postgraduate School of Librarianship and Information Science, University of Sheffield, 1967).

W L Guttsman 'Subject specialisation in academic libraries' *Journal of librarianship* 5 (1) January 1973 1-8.

J Hall 'Information services in university libraries' *Aslib proceedings* 24 (5) May 1972 293-302.

J Hall 'Survey of information services provided by British university libraries 1973 Library profiles' in *Information services in university libraries: proceedings of a Sconul seminar held at the University of Bradford, December 1973* edited by F H Ayres and J Hall (Sconul 1974) 140-208.

J Hall 'Publicity and promotion for information services in university libraries' *Aslib proceedings* 26 (10) October 1974 391-95.

K G E Harris 'The polytechnic library explosion' *New library world* 73 (855) September 1971 83-5.

K G E Harris 'Subject specialisation in polytechnic libraries: aims and objectives' *Libri* 24 (4) 1974 302-9.

K C Harrison *Public relations in libraries* (Deutsch 1973).

F Hatt 'A day in the life of a tutor-librarian' *Assistant librarian* 60 (3) March 1967 38.

F Hatt 'My kind of library tutoring' *Library Association record* 70 (10) October 1968 258-61.

C C De Winter Hebron 'Self instruction versus lecturer instruction using tape-slide in a library induction programme' *Bulletin of educational research* (7) Spring 1974 12-16.

D Holbrook 'The subject specialist in polytechnic libraries' *New library world* 73 (867) September 1972 393-6.

W R Holman *Library publications* (San Francisco, Roger Beacham, undated).

K Humphreys 'The subject specialist in national and university libraries' *Libri* 17 (1) 1967 29-41.

P B Knapp *The Monteith College library experiment* (Metuchen, New Jersey, Scarecrow Press, 1966).

P Jordan 'Behaviour in libraries' *New library world* 75 (883) January 1974 11-13 *and* 75 (884) February 1974 36-37.

'Learning today' an educational magazine of library-college thought (formerly *Library college journal*) Norman, Oklahoma 1968 8pa.

'Libraries in the new polytechnics' *Library Association record* 70 (9) September 1968 240-43.

The Library Association 'General policy statement on library resource centres in schools, colleges and institutions of higher education' *Library Association record* 75 (3) March 1973 52.

Library Association Media Cataloguing Rules Committee 'Non-book materials cataloguing rules' (National Council for Educational Technology 1973).

M B Line 'Information services in university libraries' *Journal of librarianship* 1 (4) October 1969 211-24.

M B Line 'Summing up: the information service in practice' *Aslib proceedings* 26 (1) June 1974 47-53.

H de S C MacLean 'Using the library catalogue' *New Zealand libraries* 35 (3) June 1972 165-72.

P H Mann *Students and books* (Routledge and Kegan Paul, 1974).

H Mews *Reader instruction in colleges and universities* (London, Bingley; Hamden, Conn, Linnet Books, 1972).

H Mews 'Library instruction to students at the University of Reading' *Education libraries bulletin* 32 Summer 1968 24-34.

C D Needham 'Dewey Decimal Classification' in *Reclassification: rationale and problems, proceedings of a conference . . .* edited by J M Perrault (College Park, University of Maryland School of Library and Information Sciences, 1968) 9-29.

Plan for polytechnics and other colleges: higher education in the further education system (CMND 3006) (HMSO, 1966).

K H Plate and E W Stone 'Factors affecting librarians' job satisfaction: a report on two studies' *Library quarterly* 44 (2) April 1974 97-110.

J Pratt and T Burgess *Polytechnics: a report* (Pitman, 1974).

A Pritchard and M Auckland *Book ordering and processing system study* (City of London Polytechnic, Library and Learning Resources Service, 1973).

G Renborg 'PR activities of the Stockholm Public Library' *Scandinavian public libraries quarterly* 3 (1) 1-13.

N Roberts 'Graduates in academic libraries: a survey' *Journal of librarianship* 5 (2) April 1973 97-115.

E E Robinson *The new polytechnics* (Cornmarket Press, 1968).

R D Rogers and D C Weber *University library administration* (New York, H W Wilson, 1971).

R Sergean and J R McKay 'The description and classification of jobs in librarianship and information work' *Library Association record* 76 (6) June 1974 112-15.

C A Seymour and J C Schofield 'Measuring reader failure at the catalogue' *Library resources and technical services* 17 (1) Winter 1973 6-24.

M R Shifrin *Information in the school library* (London, Bingley; Hamden, Conn, Linnet Books, 1973).

L Smart 'Graphically speaking or how do libraries sell themselves?' *Quill and quire* 40 (1) January 1974 4.

E Smith 'The impact of the subject specialist librarian on the organization and structure of the academic research library' in E I Farber and R Walling editors *The academic library: essays in honour of Guy R Lyle* (Metuchen, N J, Scarecrow Press. 1974) 71-81.

G C K Smith and J L Schofield 'A general survey of senior and intermediate staff deployment in university libraries' *Journal of librarianship* 5 (2) April 1973 97-115.

J Thompson *An introduction to university library administration* (London, Bingley; Hamden, Conn, Linnet Books, 2nd ed 1974).

M Trow 'Problems for polytechnics: an American point of view' *Universities quarterly* 23 (4) Autumn 1969 381-96.

M Trow 'Binary dilemmas: an American view' *Higher education review* 1 (3) Summer 1969 27-43.

University of Cambridge, Library Management Research Unit *Optimisation techniques in the analysis of library systems* (S C 18) (Cambridge, LMRU, University Library, 1973).

University Grants Committee, Committee on Libraries *Report* (Parry Report) (HMSO, 1967).

University of London, Committee on Library Resources *Report of the Committee...* (University of London, 1971).

University of Surrey *OSTI tape-slide evaluation project* (University of Surrey Library, 1973).

J A Urquhart and J L Schofield 'Overlap of acquisitions in the University of London libraries: a study and a methodology' *Journal of librarianship* 4 (1) January 1972 32-47.

R G Usherwood 'Library public relations: an introduction' in *Library management* Vol II edited by G Holroyd (London, Bingley; Hamden, Conn, Linnet Books, 1974).

S Williams 'Progess with the plan for the polytechnics' in *The development of the new polytechnics* (Further Education Staff College report 2 (8) 1969).

P Woodhead 'Subject specialisation in three British university libraries: a critical survey' *Libri* 24 (1) 1974 30-60.

G H Wright *The library in colleges of commerce and technology* (Deutsch, 1966).

MAY 7 1976

NSRP 179 1975

Z
675
U5
L45